Winning Interviews
for
$100,000+ Jobs

Books by Wendy Enelow...

100 Winning Resumes for $100,000+ Jobs
201 Winning Cover Letters for $100,000+ Jobs
1500+ KeyWords for $100,000+ Jobs
Resume Winners From the Pros
Winning Interviews for $100,000+ Jobs

Winning Interviews for
for
$100,000+ Jobs

Wendy Enelow, CPRW, JCTC

IMPACT PUBLICATIONS
Manassas Park, Virginia

Library of Congress Cataloging-in-Publication Data

Enelow, Wendy S.
  Winning interviews for $100,000+ jobs / Wendy Enelow
    p. cm.
  Includes index.
  ISBN 1-57023-117-6
  1. Employment interviewing. 2. Job hunting. I. Title. II.
  Title: Winning interviews for one hundred thousand dollar
  plus jobs.
  HF5549.5.I6 1999
  650.14—dc21   99-27660
                                                              CIP

Publisher: For information on Impact Publications, including current and forthcoming publications, authors, press kits, bookstore, and submission requirements, visit Impact's Web site: www.impactpublications.com

Publicity/Rights: For information on publicity, author interviews, and subsidiary rights, contact the Public Relations and Marketing Department: Tel. 703/361-7300 or Fax 703/335-9486.

Sales/Distribution: Bookstore sales are handled through Impact's trade distributor: National Book Network, 15200 NBN Way, Blue Ridge Summit, PA 17214, Tel. 1-800-462-6420. All other sales and distribution inquiries should be directed to the publisher: Sales Department, IMPACT PUBLICATIONS, 9104-N Manassas Dr., Manassas Park, VA 20111-5211, Tel. 703/361-7300, Fax 703/ 335-9486, or E-mail:winint@impactpublications.com

Book design by Kristina Ackley

Contents

1. Welcome to the World of Interviewing 1

Play To Win! 2
Powerful Performance 3
Interview Success Factors For The
 Executive Job Search Candidate 4
Interview Success Factors For The Interviewer 7
Power Words for Interview Success 10

2. Prepare to Win! 15

Formula For Success 15
Your Personal Interview Agenda 17
Interview Preparation 18
Be Prepared! 19
The Interview Process 20
Practice, Practice & Then Practice 22
First Impressions Still Count! 24
Interview Tips 25

3. Types of Interviews 29

Informational/Networking Interviews 29
Screening Interviews—Phone or Electronic 30
Hiring Interviews 33
Types of Interview Questions 37

4. Overcoming Obstacles to Opportunity 39

Interview Challenge #1—You've Been Fired! 39
Interview Challenge #2—
 You're Overqualified For Your Current Job! 41
Interview Challenge #3—
 Your Recommendations Are Poor! 43

Interview Challenge #4—
   You Haven't Worked For A Year!   45
Interview Challenge #5—It's Someone Else's Agenda!   47

5. **Winning Answers to Tough Interview Questions   49**
You Can Win!   49
The Forbidden Fruit   82
Questions You Should Ask   85

6. **Negotiating Winning Compensation Plans 87**
Negotiating & Accepting The Offer   90
Salary, Benefits & Your Compensation Plan   92
Executive Employment Contracts   97

7. **Winning Follow-Up Strategies 103**
Power Thank You Letters   103
Sample Thank You Letters   104
Winning Telephone Follow-Up Strategies   111
Leverage Your Contact Network   112

8. **Tips from the Top 114**

9. **Winning in the Next Millennium 140**
My Challenge To You   142

Career Resources 149

Winning Interviews
for
$100,000+ Jobs

1
Welcome to the World of Interviewing

It's 9:15 a.m. and you've been sitting in the reception area for 20 minutes now, waiting for them to call you. You're nervous. This is a big interview, the biggest of your life. The opportunity is ideal for you. With more than 15 years' experience as CFO with a mid-size information technology company, you're now poised to take the helm as Treasurer of this Fortune 500 company. You know the competition is fierce. Yet you've already made it to round #4 in the interview process; you know they are considering only three other candidates at this point and you feel reasonably confident.

But this is your last chance. You know that today—in front of the entire Executive Committee and Board of Directors—you must impress them or you'll never get back in the door again. This is it. Even though you know you are extremely well qualified and would excel in the position, you are apprehensive. On the outside you're calm and collected; on the inside, your heart is beating fast, your pulse is racing and your mind is going a million miles a second. There is so much you want to be sure to communicate. Can you remember it all? Will you present yourself well? Can you demonstrate that you really can be a valuable asset to the management team, the Board and the company?

Just then the receptionist walks up and asks you to follow. Slowly, you both make your way down two long corridors and walk into a brightly lit conference room. There are 12 of them—8 men and 4 women—all eyeing you as you walk in, greet them each individually and take your seat. What tremendous power and control these 12 people hold today—people who are probably no more qualified nor more successful than you. Your destiny is in their hands.

PLAY TO WIN!

Do those 12 people really have all of the control? To some degree, yes. Ultimately, these 12 individuals will make a hiring decision that will, in the short term, significantly impact your career and perhaps your self-esteem. You know you are qualified, you know you can perform well beyond their expectations and you know that your references are excellent. Today's most significant challenge is to build rapport and trust, and to begin to immerse yourself into the company's culture and its inner circle.

But you have power too. What transpires in that conference room is largely up to you. Will you be in control of the interview? Will you be effective in communicating information regarding your professional experience, skills, achievements and personal attributes that are so critical to demonstrating your ability and distinguishing yourself from the other candidates? Will you be able to start to build the relationships today that will be vital to your selection and your ultimate success?

Yes, you can. If you are an educated job seeker with strong interviewing skills, you already know that YOU have the control and the power to shape your own destiny. You walked into that conference room with your own personal agenda—information to communicate, skills to demonstrate, problem solving competencies to highlight and successes that validate it all. Your goal is to keep the interview heading in a positive direction, providing you with the opportunity to communicate that which is most important. You must keep your mind focused, your senses alert and your responses to their questions right on target. Your physical appearance and demeanor must be sharp; you must communicate your high level of personal integrity and ethics. It's all up to you. Are you ready for the challenge? Can you win at the interviewing game?

POWERFUL PERFORMANCE

For many individuals this type of interview situation can be extremely intimidating. It's not just you and the Human Resources Manager sitting comfortably in a private office discussing your past experiences and interest in the company. It's not just you and the retiring Treasurer exploring the specific job responsibilities. It's not just you and the CEO chatting about the company's needs, vision and long-term objectives. These situations would be much more comfortable, easier to manage and less threatening. Rather, it is a situation where 12 top executives are scrutinizing you, listening to every word you say and watching every move you make. Why wouldn't you be a bit intimidated and nervous?

The stress you feel in this interview or any other type of interview situation is not only normal, it's useful. The adrenaline flowing through your body makes you sharper, more alert and more focused. One of the world's most renowned opera singers has said that after more than 20 years on the stage, as she waits behind the curtain before each performance, she feels the stress, the nervousness and the energy. It is what excites her and pushes her to perform. The same can be said about interviewing. If you can harness the energy and push it in a positive direction, it will give you power.

Think of your interview just like that—a platform on which to perform. You're in the spotlight and you've got an agenda to communicate to your audience. The energy rushing through your body is simply stage fright that, when harnessed, will give you the strength, the intensity and the power to win over your audience.

> Stress can be a **positive** reaction to interviewing if you channel that energy in the right direction.

INTERVIEW SUCCESS FACTORS FOR THE EXECUTIVE JOB SEARCH CANDIDATE

When you enter an interview situation, you must be prepared with your own agenda—critical messages you wish to communicate to your interviewer. For the executive job seeker, these must include the following:

```
I   N        T     E          R       V         I          E        W
    integrity          enthusiasm         vitality          educated        in
        negotiate          rapport             innovative
            trust
```

I **Integrity**—The thought may be trite, but people want to hire people who are honorable, ethical and have a high level of personal integrity. When you are employed by an organization, particularly in a senior executive position, you represent the company in everything that you do. In any interview, your #1 objective is to communicate that message to a prospective employer. Let him/her know that he/she can trust in your integrity and your word.

N **Negotiate**—Your ability to negotiate will be critical throughout the entire interview process. Not only will you be negotiating your salary, bonus structure, benefits and total compensation package (see Chapter 6); you will be negotiating for an opportunity. Look at interviewing as a unique negotiation between two parties working to achieve consensus. Your objective is to bring the interviewer over to your "side of the table" and win the job offer.

T **Trust**—Building trust with your interviewer is critical. To be embraced by a company, there must be an immediate sense of trust between all parties. Be honest and above board with all of your answers, working hard to position them positively, but remaining truthful. If, for whatever reason, you are not able to build a sense of trust, chances are the interview will not result in a second interview or an offer.

E **Enthusiasm**—No one wants to hire someone who is lackadaisical, unmotivated and "just there." Your challenge in any interview situation is to demonstrate your enthusiasm—for the position, for the company and for the opportunity. Enter the interview with excitement, a smile and a spring in your step, and the entire atmosphere will be energized. You feel it and so will your interviewer, leaving a long lasting, positive impression.

R **Rapport**—Building rapport with your interviewer is vital. No interviewer is going to recommend a second interview or make an employment offer to an individual that he/she feels uncomfortable with. Be sure that one of the most important items on your interview agenda is developing rapport with your interviewer.

V **Vitality**—Demonstrate a sense of energy, drive and enthusiasm every step of the way in the interview process. Companies want to hire individuals who are vital, dynamic, self-motivated and driven to succeed. Be sure that you communicate that message. This is particularly true for older interview candidates who must—right or wrong—demonstrate that they are vital, youthful and competent, not "over the hill" executives.

I Innovative—The employment market is more competitive than ever before. To give yourself an edge over other candidates, you must demonstrate your innovation. This can include specific achievements, project highlights, processes you have redesigned and improved, problems you have solved, new products you have developed, new revenue streams you have created, and your specific contributions to bottom-line profitability. Utilize your career success to demonstrate innovation and results.

E Educated—Communicate the fact that you are well educated, either through formal training and/or life experiences. Companies want to hire individuals who are well-versed in their chosen profession and industry. Demonstrate your knowledge through your resume, your conversation and your ease in presentation style. If you have attended professional training and executive development programs, share that information. If you have led non-profit organizations, spoken at national conferences, written for trade publications and the like, share that information. All of this serves to further validate your qualifications and your credibility.

W Win—Bottom-line, in any interview situation, your objective is to win the next interview, win the support of your interviewer, and ultimately, win the opportunity. Interviewing can be a stressful situation, fraught with pitfalls to exclude you from consideration. Consider it one of life's most challenging games. Your goal is to win against the competition and get the offer—even if you do not ultimately accept the position. Never let this thought leave you.

INTERVIEW SUCCESS FACTORS FOR THE INTERVIEWER

When an HR Executive, hiring manager or other individuals interview you, they have their own agenda—part personal and part on behalf of the company. Not only must you stick with your own agenda, you must be responsive to theirs.

I N T E R V I E W
nvestigate
otice
ranscend
xclude
esearch
alidate
nterrogate
xtrapolate
ise Decisions

I   **Investigate**—The interviewer's #1 objective is to *"investigate"* who you are, the qualifications you bring to the company, your level of competency within specific skill sets and other information relevant to the particular opportunity at hand. Interviewing is exploration to uncover the facts.

N   **Notice**—An interviewer's challenge is to notice everything about you that is clearly, and sometimes not so clearly, obvious. It may be your ability to make eye contact, your firm handshake, your style of dress, your personal hygiene, the length of your hair, how you sit, how you walk, where your hands are when you stand, your personal handwriting and much more. The interviewer takes mental notes throughout the process and then clearly documents all of this information.

T   **Transcend**—One of the greatest challenges facing each interviewer is the ability to transcend what you are saying so as to understand the *"real"* message. Here's an example. Suppose the interviewer inquires about your experience in personnel training, development and direct supervision. The reality may be that you have none, but you certainly don't want to communicate that message. Instead, you might say ... "Throughout my career, I have always worked with cross-functional, cross-departmental project teams. My role has been to coordinate project assignments, scheduling, reporting and administration for groups of up to 35 personnel. This has been particularly challenging in our environment where there has been a tremendous hiring influx and the need for ongoing job training and support." If the interviewer is able to effectively transcend, he/she will realize that what you've really said is "No."

E Exclude—Believe it or not, one of the primary objectives of an interviewer (particularly in phase #1 of the interview process) is to exclude potential candidates and the number of individuals moving on to phase #2. Feel comfort in the fact that if the interviewer or company did not believe that you had the basic qualifications, you would not be interviewing. So, you're already past the preliminary screening. Go into the interview with a sense of accomplishment thus far and confidence in your abilities. However, if, after this stage, you are excluded for whatever reason, let it go. All too often job seekers work to recapture an opportunity that, for whatever reason, has been lost. If the interviewer does not believe you to be an appropriate candidate, it is extremely unlikely that you can change his/her mind no matter what you say or do.

R Research—Be advised that the interviewer and/or the company will closely research your background— whatever they can find out and from whomever. Of course, at some point, they will contact your references, but many companies go well beyond basic reference checking. Remember, the higher the level of position, the closer the scrutiny. Can you withstand this type of research into your background—personal and professional?

V **Validate**—At some point in the process, the interviewer (or someone else within the company) will be responsible for validating the information you have presented in your resume and during the interview. Be sure that you have been 100% honest and accurate in your presentation of ALL the facts—employment history, educational qualifications, technical skills, project highlights, quantifiable results and more. If, during the company's background check, they are unable to validate the information that you have provided, you have lost and can never recapture the opportunity.

I **Interrogate**—Although this may seem a bit harsh, an interviewer's goal is to interrogate, questioning you, your skills, experiences, competencies, achievements, successes, project highlights and more. The task at hand for them is to delve as deeply as possible into your career history to explore all of the qualifications you bring to that position. Do not be threatened, but rather view the interrogation as an opportunity.

E **Extrapolate**—Any qualified interviewer comes to each interview with a specific agenda regarding information that he/she wants from you relative to your skills, experiences and competencies. In turn, they will have developed targeted questions and points of conversation to extrapolate that specific information. Be advised that you always want to answer each and every question in full, but that your challenge is to also address your own agenda (the information you believe is important to communicate).

W   Wise Decisions—Ultimately, at any stage in the executive interview process, the interviewer is challenged to make wise decisions. Should this candidate be excluded for any particular reason? Should this candidate be invited back for another interview, further up in the chain of command? Should we make an offer to this candidate? What are the risks involved in hiring this individual? Provide your interviewer with solid information, verifiable results and a strong track record of performance, and you will strengthen his/her decision-making ability. Remember, a key indicator of interview success is the relationship you build with the interviewer and what reflection that will have upon him/her and his/her hiring performance.

POWER WORDS FOR INTERVIEW SUCCESS

The following three lists of power words and phrases will allow you to create a sense of energy, excitement and success in your interviews. Use these key words as appropriate to communicate your skills, qualifications, achievements and track record of performance. Do not simply throw them into the conversation, but rather use them to highlight specific positions, responsibilities, projects, challenges and accomplishments.

Executive Skill Sets

Review the following list carefully and highlight the items that match your skills, career history and achievements. Then integrate them as appropriate into your interview communications. Note that many of these skills are key qualifications for virtually any executive position.

- ☐ Benchmarking & Best-in-Class Practices
- ☐ Board Relations & Presentations

- ☐ Business Planning
- ☐ Change Management
- ☐ Competitive Negotiations & Wins
- ☐ Corporate, Customer & Employee Communications
- ☐ Cost Reduction & Avoidance
- ☐ Customer Service, Retention & Loyalty
- ☐ Efficiency Improvement
- ☐ Executive Leadership
- ☐ Fast-Track Promotion
- ☐ Financial Control
- ☐ Financial Leadership
- ☐ Global Expansion & Diversification
- ☐ High-Growth Organizations
- ☐ International Business Affairs
- ☐ Joint Ventures, Partnerships & Strategic Alliances
- ☐ Market Expansion & Diversification
- ☐ Market Image & Perception
- ☐ Market Share Increases
- ☐ Mergers & Acquisitions
- ☐ Multinational Organizations
- ☐ New Venture Development & Launch
- ☐ Organizational Development & Leadership
- ☐ PC & Internet Proficiency
- ☐ Performance Improvement & Management
- ☐ Process Redesign & Simplification
- ☐ Product Design, Development & Commercialization
- ☐ Productivity Improvement
- ☐ Profit & Loss Management
- ☐ Profit & Revenue Improvement
- ☐ Quality Improvement
- ☐ Relationship Building & Management
- ☐ ROA, ROE & ROI Gains
- ☐ Shareholder & Stakeholder Value
- ☐ Start-Up Enterprises & Ventures
- ☐ Strategic Planning & Vision
- ☐ Success & Results

- ☐ Total Quality Management
- ☐ Transition Management
- ☐ Turnaround & Revitalization
- ☐ World Class Operations

Personal & Professional Characteristics

Review the following list carefully and highlight the items that match your personal and professional characteristics. Then integrate them as appropriate into your interview communications. Note that many of these characteristics are vital to executive recruitment and selection.

☐ Accomplished	☐ Loyal
☐ Adaptable	☐ Market-Driven
☐ Analytical	☐ Mature
☐ Assertive	☐ Methodical
☐ Authentic	☐ Motivated
☐ Believable	☐ Multilingual
☐ Bold	☐ Nurturing
☐ Charismatic	☐ Objective
☐ Competent	☐ Observant
☐ Competitive	☐ Organized
☐ Conceptual	☐ Perceptive
☐ Confident	☐ Persevering
☐ Conscientious	☐ Persistent
☐ Courageous	☐ Personable
☐ Creative	☐ Persuasive
☐ Credible	☐ Poised
☐ Customer-Driven	☐ Polished
☐ Decisive	☐ Positive
☐ Dedicated	☐ Practical

- ☐ Dependable
- ☐ Determined
- ☐ Devoted
- ☐ Diligent
- ☐ Diplomatic
- ☐ Direct
- ☐ Dynamic
- ☐ Earnest
- ☐ Effective
- ☐ Efficient
- ☐ Eloquent
- ☐ Encouraging
- ☐ Energized
- ☐ Enterprising
- ☐ Enthusiastic
- ☐ Entrepreneurial
- ☐ Ethical
- ☐ Expressive
- ☐ Flexible
- ☐ Honest
- ☐ Honorable
- ☐ Humanitarian
- ☐ Imaginative
- ☐ Independent
- ☐ Industrious
- ☐ Ingenious
- ☐ Insightful
- ☐ Intelligent

- ☐ Pragmatic
- ☐ Precise
- ☐ Prepared
- ☐ Productive
- ☐ Proud
- ☐ Prudent
- ☐ Reputable
- ☐ Resilient
- ☐ Resourceful
- ☐ Responsive
- ☐ Savvy
- ☐ Sharp
- ☐ Sophisticated
- ☐ Stalwart
- ☐ Strategic
- ☐ Strong
- ☐ Subjective
- ☐ Successful
- ☐ Supportive
- ☐ Tactful
- ☐ Tactical
- ☐ Talented
- ☐ Tenacious
- ☐ Thorough
- ☐ Tolerant
- ☐ Trustworthy
- ☐ Vigorous
- ☐ Visionary

☐ Intense   ☐ Vital

☐ Intuitive   ☐ Wise

Personality & Style Descriptors

Review the following list carefully and highlight the items that best describe your personality and style. Then integrate them as appropriate into your interview communications. Note that many of these characteristics are vital to executive recruitment and selection.

☐ Advocate   ☐ Leader

☐ Catalyst   ☐ Listener

☐ Champion   ☐ Manager

☐ Coach   ☐ Mediator

☐ Confidante   ☐ Mentor

☐ Consensus Builder   ☐ Negotiator

☐ Decision Maker   ☐ Pioneer

☐ Delegator   ☐ Problem Solver

☐ Driver   ☐ Team Builder

☐ Influencer   ☐ Troubleshooter

☐ Innovator   ☐ Winner

2

Prepare to Win!

Once you have devoted the time and energy to planning your search strategy, developing your marketing tools (resumes, cover letters, broadcast letters) and launching your career marketing program, you're ready for the next step—INTERVIEWING TO WIN!

Formula For Success

There are four basic ingredients to getting the job that you apply for. Each is vital to your success throughout each and every phase of the interview process. Each will be directly compared to those of your competitors, other individuals applying for, and qualified for, the same position. To win, you must demonstrate your competency and excel in your performance in all four areas.

1. **Your qualifications on paper**—the content and appearance of your resume, cover letter, application and other written communications.
2. **Your attitude and behavior**.
3. **Your references** and what they say about your performance, qualifications, achievements, personality, behavior and interpersonal skills.
4. **Your personal performance in the interview**.

With the first two, you have virtually total control. The time and effort you invest in developing your resume and cover letter is directly proportionate to the number and quality of interviews you are offered. Your attitude and behavior are equally important. Companies want to hire winners who are confident of their ability to perform and deliver positive results. They want to hire individuals who are excited about their organization, energetic, full of new ideas and strategies, and able to quickly build camaraderie with the other members of the executive team and their staffs. They want to hire success. If you can communicate a positive attitude, you have won half the battle.

What your references have to say about you is, to some degree, not within your control. However, it is assumed that you have given considerable thought to your selection of references and are confident that each will communicate positive messages about your performance, qualifications, capabilities and value to a prospective employer.

Where references can become more difficult to manage is when a prospective employer contacts your current or most recent employer and you have left, or are planning to leave, that position under less than favorable circumstances. In this situation, it can be difficult to anticipate what an individual will say about you. If you are concerned that their comments may be negative, it is highly recommended that you address that issue in the interview, prior to your references being contacted. If you bring up the topic, tell your interviewer that you are leaving your current position (or left your past position) because it has not been a positive experience, and explain why, you have a much greater chance of overcoming this obstacle than if you simply ignore it and leave your interviewer to discover this on his/her own when the effects can be quite negative. This does not mean that you should lie or misrepresent. Rather, you should attempt to position the information in the most favorable light possible considering the circumstances. For more information on dealing with difficult situations, refer to the section on *"Overcoming Obstacles To Opportunity"* in Chapter 4.

References have become a *"tricky"* thing today. Many companies offer little more than your job title and dates of employment for fear of litigation. If they were to give an honest appraisal of your performance, the slightest thing could be misinterpreted, you could lose the opportunity and potentially bring legal action against them. Companies are often scared to say anything of substance—good or bad.

The strength of your interviewing skills and your ability to communicate a positive message of success, achievement and performance are perhaps the most vital to your success and a key factor in positioning yourself against the competition. If you do not perform well in the interview situation, no matter your qualifications, chances are likely that you will not be offered the position. Conversely, even if you are not the most qualified candidate, but are the best at interviewing, chances are the position will be yours.

YOUR PERSONAL INTERVIEW AGENDA

What is your personal agenda for the interview? There are three primary agenda items that should drive you throughout the entire interview process.

As has been and will be repeated in this book over and over, job search is **marketing**. You have a product to sell—YOURSELF. Your challenge is to effectively market, merchandise, advertise and promote that product to the right audience. And one of the most critical components of your marketing campaign is your ability to favorably present that product in an interview situation. How can you best highlight the features and benefits of the product? What are the successes and achievements of the product? What is the value of the product to me and my company? Why do I want to *"buy"* this product?

The interview platform is yours to answer the questions above and many others. To succeed, you must know that your product is the best and not be afraid to promote it. Job search and interviewing are tremendously competitive today. Those who win not only have the qualifications, but also the confidence in themselves to sell what it is that they have accomplished and what they bring to the table.

Equally important to your interview success is your ability to demonstrate your **honesty and integrity**. Be truthful in responding to all interview questions and never provide your interviewer with the opportunity to question your ethics. Demonstrate, through your answers, that you have faced difficult ethical questions and issues in the past, and that you have always maintained your personal level of integrity. No one wants to hire an individual whose honesty and behavior are questionable.

The third and perhaps most critical item on your agenda is quite simple—**a job offer**. Unless this is an informational interview or networking interview, and not a hiring interview, your primary objective is a job offer. And not just a job offer, but a well-compensated offer. This agenda item should be the catalyst throughout your entire job search process and during each interview. There is really no reason to accept an invitation for an interview unless you are seriously seeking an offer.

Remember, however, that offers for executive employment are almost never made during interview #1. Offers will be forthcoming further in the process, after you have learned more about the company and the position, and the company has had the opportunity to learn more about you, your skills, qualifications, achievements and value to their organization.

INTERVIEW PREPARATION

To prepare for an interview, you must:

- Remember that interviewing is selling. You are there to promote a product—YOURSELF—highlight its features and benefits, and position yourself for a new career opportunity.

- Research everything that you can about the company you will be interviewing with and the position you will be interviewing for.

- Appear confident and enthusiastic with a high level of energy and impeccable ethics.

- Dress the part of the executive, act the part and display the appropriate behaviors.

- Remember that interviewing is a two-way street. Not only is the company interviewing you, you are also interviewing them. Will you be proud to work for this company? Do you like the environment? Do you like the people? What are the long-term opportunities?

- Remember that the interviewer's primary goal during interview #1 is to identify prime candidates and eliminate unqualified ones.

- Remember that your primary objective in interview #1 is an invitation for interview #2. Your secondary objective in interview #1 and all subsequent interviews is, of course, a job offer.

Your **objective** in interview #1 is straightforward—
an invitation for interview #2

BE PREPARED!

Materials You Will Need

Arrive at each interview with either a leather portfolio or briefcase that contains:

- additional copies of your resume
- letters of recommendation and referral
- copies of outstanding performance reviews
- copies of a select number of honors and awards

- press clippings (features & articles you authored)
- a plain pad of paper for note taking
- at least three pens
- your current business cards (if applicable)

It's Okay To Take Notes!

Not only is it okay to take notes, it is strongly recommended. When you take a moment to jot down a few thoughts, you are demonstrating your interest in the company and the position. You are showing your interviewer that you are really listening to what he/she is saying.

Furthermore, these notes will be the foundation for your subsequent thank you letter which is discussed in detail in Chapter 7. At this point, let it suffice to say that your thank you letter is really a marketing tool and is best referred to as a "power" thank you letter. Of course you want to express your appreciation, but more importantly, you want to clearly reiterate the qualifications you bring to the position based upon the company's specific needs. For example, if during the interview there was a great deal of discussion regarding the instability of the workforce, you would then comment in your power thank you letter how you have met this challenge in the past. Note taking during the interview session will help you remember issues that were addressed, problems the company is facing and challenges to be met.

The greatest benefit of power thank you letters is their ability to distinguish you from other candidates who pass along the more traditional thank you letter. With your power letter, you've demonstrated a sincere interest in the organization and perhaps offered some solutions. Your interviewer and the company will be intrigued.

THE INTERVIEW PROCESS

The interview process is generally initiated through your efforts in contacting a company or a recruiter. Either you are aware of a specific opportunity, have been recommended by one of your network contacts or simply contacted the organization to express your interest in executive employment opportunities. Your contact will sometimes begin with a telephone call; other times, by forwarding your resume and cover letter.

Once the company or recruiter has received your materials, they will be closely reviewed. Do you have the qualifications for the position they advertised or for an anticipated future opportunity? Are you the type of individual they would be interested in interviewing and perhaps hiring? Do you present a unique set of skills and qualifications? Do you have contacts that may be of value to the organization? Is the company anticipating growth and expansion, dictating the need for additional executive talent? Is one of their current executives planning to retire or leave the company shortly?

If the company's answer to any of the above questions is yes, and they are impressed by your written qualifications, chances are the next step will be a preliminary interview in the form of a telephone screening. This is particularly true for candidates who live out-of-state. Prior to the company investing money to bring you in for a personal interview, an initial telephone screening will generally be conducted to further determine that (1) you have the *"right"* qualifications and (2) you have the *"right"* attitude, personality and characteristics.

If you pass the initial telephone screening, a date and time for a personal interview will be scheduled. Refer to Chapter 3, *"Types of Interviews"* to learn about the various interview scenarios that may present themselves. You can think of the telephone screening as a preliminary test to determine if you possess the skills, qualifications and experiences that the company is seeking in a qualified candidate. You can assume that if you pass this phase of the interview process, you will be invited for a face-to-face interview.

How many interviews can you expect before an offer is put on the table? That is a very difficult question to answer. There may be instances where, after only two interviews, you are presented with an offer. However, considering the level of position you are seeking as a senior executive, it is more likely that there will be multiple interviews long before an offer is ever made.

Virtually every senior management and executive job seeker can expect to interview with other senior executives of the hiring company. This would include the CEO, President, CFO, Human Resources Director and perhaps Executive Vice Presidents of specific operating functions (e.g., Sales, Marketing, Manufacturing, Customer Service, Product Development, Administration, Information Technology). You may also be asked to interview with members of or the entire Board of Directors, the company's bankers or their investor group, their strategic business partners and others with a vested interest. Obviously, the more senior the position, the more intense and widespread the interview process becomes.

Practice, Practice & Then Practice

How many individuals can walk into an interview situation poised, relaxed and confident in their ability? For individuals who are naturally charming, interesting and comfortable in what can be somewhat *"threatening"* situations, interviews are generally no problem. These individuals tend to have strong communication and interpersonal relations skills, and naturally exude confidence and success.

Most people, however, are not natural charmers and more often than not, are intimidated in an interview situation. This is particularly true if they have been in the job market for an extended period of time, are beginning to feel the financial impact, and starting to question their own value and self-worth. It is a natural inclination to be anxious before the interview (you really need this job!) and begin to question your own qualifications (why has no one hired me yet?).

Performing well in an interview does not mean changing who you are. Rather, it means that you must clearly identify and work to minimize your weaknesses in this type of situation. The first step in this process is to be honest with yourself. Are you confident in an interview? Can you answer the difficult questions? Can you overcome objections? Can you competitively position yourself against other candidates? Can you play to win?

To overcome these obstacles and become a more polished and confident interviewer, practice is essential. Just as with any other task, you can positively influence and enhance your performance and results through preparation and rehearsal. Practice will help you to become much better organized and clearer in your thought process, providing you with the knowledge to answer the expected questions correctly and with confidence.

Being a bit nervous in an interview situation is expected. In fact, the adrenaline gives you the energy and the edge to perform. Ask any stage actor or theatrical performer. They will tell you that they continue to experience stage fright even after years of live performances, but have learned to harness that anxiety into positive energy. Interview situations are much the same. Realize that the nervousness sharpens your senses and can be the catalyst for one of your best performances ever.

For practice interviews, you can ask a friend, relative or colleague for assistance. You want to simulate an interview situation as closely as possible by creating a physical environment much like that of an interview—a private area or room with desk or table and two chairs. Forget that you know each other and begin the practice session with a welcoming handshake and a few brief moments of light conversation, much as you will experience in an actual interview.

Then use the interview questions in Chapter 5 as your practice guide.

You might also consider approaching another professional who is currently in an active job search campaign to be your interview practice partner. This is a great way for both of you to have the opportunity to practice, brainstorm and refine each other's interview performance.

Finally, if you believe that your interviewing skills require major surgery, consider hiring a career counselor or coach. These individuals are well trained in interviewing and can provide you with substantive feedback and direction to enhance your performance. For an investment of only a few hundred dollars, a counselor or coach can often make a dramatic difference in your interview success and, in turn, the number of offers you will receive.

Whomever you select as your interview partner, it is imperative that you devote the time and energy that is necessary to fine tune your interviewing skills and your answers. Go over questions time and time again until you feel confident in your responses, the messages you convey and the manner in which you communicate. Rehearsals are great. You can stop and start as many times as you may like until your answers are second nature. With real interviews you do not have that luxury so make sure that you are better than 100% prepared.

First Impressions Still Count!

All of our lives we've been taught that first impressions count and leave a lasting impression. Nowhere is this more apparent than in the job search and interview process. In these situations, first impressions are vital and based on four specific observations:

1. **Punctuality**. If you're late, you're usually out of the running. There are virtually no excuses for late arrivals (barring any unforeseen emergencies). Give

yourself plenty of time and then some. In fact, arriving a few minutes early allows you the opportunity to collect your thoughts, take a deep breath, relax and get ready.

2. **Appropriate business attire**. Modern yet conservative clothing is the recommendation—nothing too flashy or faddish. When your interviewer takes his/ her first glance, you want them to note that you are sharp, classy and a cut above the competition.

3. **Personal grooming habits**. Scraggly beards, unkempt hair and nose piercings are out of the question! Need I say more?

4. **Self-confidence** (*"controlled nervousness"*). A warm smile, direct eye contact and a firm handshake make a positive and lasting impression.

If you make a good first impression, your interview will get off to a positive start. However, if your first impression is less than desirable, most likely you have lost the opportunity.

INTERVIEW TIPS

Following are the nine top strategic and tactical tips to enhance your interviewing skills, allowing you to outperform your competition and position yourself for an outstanding executive opportunity. Read these tips carefully and be sure to integrate them, as appropriate, into your responses to each and every interview question.

1. **Sell it to me ... don't tell it to me**. Interviewing is basically a selling game. You have a product to promote—YOURSELF—and your goal is to market that product as effectively as possible. Don't just tell the interviewer that "Yes, I managed annual budgeting for the division." Rather, SELL the fact that "For the

past six years I have managed the entire budgeting function for a $22 million operating division, initiated a series of cost reduction programs and cut $2.5 million from the bottom-line." You've sold the success, not just told the facts!

2. **Transition each negative to a positive**. Suppose someone inquires as to your proficiency with Excel. You know that you have never touched the program. However, you certainly do not want to blurt out, "No, I'm not familiar with it." Rather, transition the negative to a positive with the following. "I have used spreadsheet applications throughout my career and am most familiar with Lotus. I'm sure getting a good handle on Excel won't take long at all."

3. **Use the *"big to little strategy."*** Putting some structure into your interview responses will make the process much easier, more manageable and more effective. Begin your answers with a "BIG" response and then use specific "LITTLE" examples to demonstrate your proficiency. Consider the following example. Your interviewer inquires about your experience in managing information technology resources. Your response begins with "Throughout the past 12 years, I have held full strategic planning, operating and management responsibility for a 48-person information resources organization." Then onto the little, "Specific highlights that may interest you include a $3.8 million investment in client/server hardware, introduction of both Internet and Intranet technologies, and the successful start-up of a global telecommunications network."

4. **Use function to demonstrate scope of responsibility and achievement.** If your interviewer inquires about your daily functional responsibility as Senior Director of Human Resources, do not just provide a

laundry list of tasks. Rather, use this opportunity to communicate the scope of your responsibility. For example, "As HR Director, I managed the entire personnel function for a 2200-employee corporation. I introduced new compensation plans throughout six manufacturing locations, created a unique incentive program for all levels of management, negotiated favorable union contracts governing over 90% of our workforce, and facilitated the acquisition and introduction of PeopleSoft to enhance our information technology capabilities."

5. **Be confident in the fact that you've already passed the first test**. If you are interviewing in a face-to-face situation, be confident that you have already passed the preliminary review of your skills, qualifications and experience. If you hadn't, you would not have been invited for the interview. Therefore, enter the interview situation with enthusiasm and security in the fact that you have the basic qualifications. Now your challenge is to sell, negotiate, close and win!

6. **Remain in the realm of reality**. Everyone pushes the envelope a bit when interviewing. You're there to promote yourself, sell your success, highlight your achievements and get a job offer. However, always live by the motto, *"Remain in the realm of reality."* Every single thing you communicate on your resume or in an interview must be 100% accurate, truthful and verifiable. Only push so far. If you go beyond reality, you will have lost the opportunity.

7. **Take the initiative**. If there is information that you believe is important to communicate to your interviewer, be sure to take the initiative and introduce the topic into the conversation when appropriate. If you are nearing the end of your interview and the topic has never been addressed, tell your interviewer

that there are several other points you would like to address and inquire if now would be the appropriate time. If you don't take the initiative, chances are you will lose the opportunity to raise the topic.

8. **Be positive, confident and self-assured.** Companies want to hire winners and winners communicate an immediate message of confidence in their abilities. Be sure that you convey this message through both your verbal and non-verbal communications. A strong handshake, direct eye contact and a smile readily communicate self-assurance and poise.

9. **Listen carefully.** In any interview situation, you are there to answer questions, provide information, explore the opportunity, highlight your success and market your qualifications. However, just as important, you are there to listen to your interviewer, understand his/her concerns and directly respond to those issues. This can be a difficult challenge because so much of your energy is focused on answering the interviewer's questions as opposed to hearing what the interviewer is saying.

   Your interviewer will most likely communicate a great deal of information about the position, the company, the major issues impacting the company, the need to fill the position and the qualifications for the ideal candidate. Listen carefully to all of this information. Then use it wisely in positioning your responses, and later, in writing your power thank you letter. If your interviewer knows that you are *"hearing"* what he/she is saying, you will clearly demonstrate a message of interest and commitment. People want to hire other people who understand them, support them and are sensitive to their needs. Position yourself above the crowd by not only communicating your competencies, but responding to the organization's specific needs.

3

Types of Interviews

Now that you have devoted the necessary time and energy to preparing for your interviews, practicing your answers and refining your presentation style, you are ready to move forward. You can anticipate encountering three basic types of interviews during your job search:

- Informational/Networking Interviews
- Screening Interviews
- Hiring Interviews

Each has a unique purpose and strategy; each affords you the opportunity to market yourself, sell your achievements and position yourself for a challenging new executive opportunity.

INFORMATIONAL/NETWORKING INTERVIEWS

These types of interviews are often overlooked, but can be a valuable tool in the initial planning and development stages of your executive job search program. Informational and networking interviews provide you with the opportunity to explore new career paths, professions, industries and markets by meeting with/speaking with individuals directly involved in those disciplines. Most significant, you want to uncover the specific skills, qualifications and competencies that such companies require of their executive candidates. It is a time of exploration, research and information collection to provide you with the background critical to identifying *"how"* you want to position yourself, *"where"* you want to position yourself and *"who"* you want to be. These interviews can also be a springboard for direct referrals to specific opportunities.

Similar to when you are building your personal network of contacts, approach these types of interviews with a query for help and assistance—NOT a specific job. And, just as with your other networking efforts, allow your market reach to be broad. Contact friends, relatives, acquaintances, colleagues, co-workers, managers and even strangers to identify opportunities for networking or informational interviews. Although these individuals may not have a direct lead or opportunity, each has his/her own personal network of contacts that you can leverage to further expand and accelerate your campaign.

Never think that informational and networking interviews are a waste of time. In addition to providing you with information regarding new industries, positions and career opportunities, these types of interviews can result in formal job interviews (if an opportunity exists), a referral to someone else within that individual's company or a referral to an outside contact.

SCREENING INTERVIEWS—PHONE OR ELECTRONIC

Screening interviews are just what they imply. A particular job opportunity exists and step #1 in the company's interview process is to screen potential candidates either in or out of consideration. These types of interviews have become a norm in today's competitive market where it is not unusual for a company to receive 200, 500, 700 or even a 1000 resumes in response to a specific opportunity, many of which are from applicants nationwide. The interviewer's goal is to review resumes, select candidates who meet the company's basic hiring requirements for that specific opportunity, and then conduct preliminary interviews to ascertain if, indeed, an individual has the right qualifications and is the type of candidate the company is seeking. Screening interviews are a quick, efficient and low cost strategy for companies to narrow their list of applicants to just a select few to be brought in for face-to-face interviews. They are usually short in duration, dictated by a specific set of questions and have one objective in mind—exclusion of inappropriate candidates.

Screening interviews can be conducted via telephone, in-person or through the use of electronic technology. The higher the level of position you are seeking, the more likely that you will be screened either by phone or in person. These types of interviews not only give your interviewer specific information regarding your skills, performance, employment history and competencies, but also allow the interviewer to get a sense of who you are, how you communicate, how you interact, and if you might *"fit"* into their corporate culture. Technology-based screenings (via a PC, the Internet or email) are generally for younger, less experienced personnel where screening is based largely on specific skills and measurable qualifications. These types of screening interviews are totally unbiased, asking the exact same questions in the same tone of voice and in the same order to each and every potential hire. Further, the computer can instantaneously score your answers and determine whether or not you should be asked to proceed with the interview process.

Bear in mind that these types of screening interviews are not the norm for senior executives, although as technology continues to expand, it is inevitable that they will become a more widely used executive screening tool.

If a prospective employer phones you to obtain additional information, you can assume that this is a screening interview. Treat it seriously, as you would any other interview.

What information you communicate to this individual (despite the limited amount of time), how it is presented, your tone, your attitude and your energy are all important considerations as to whether or not you will be invited for a personal interview.

Most of these calls will come unexpectedly. To ensure that you are ALWAYS prepared, keep a working space available right by your telephone. Not only will you need paper and pen, it is advisable that you keep an index card file readily accessible. This file should contain the names and addresses of all of your job contacts, information about available positions, dates you forwarded your resume and cover letter, and other specific information. Also keep a copy of your resume available for quick and easy reference. Do not allow a prospective employer to ever catch you unprepared. If you do, chances are you will lose the opportunity.

If you are invited for a face-to-face screening interview, you will most likely be meeting with one of the company's human resource professionals or with an outside recruiter. The agenda is the same as if completed on the telephone—to get basic information and determine whether or not you have the qualifications required for the position. A face-to-face interview is a much more valuable preliminary tool, allowing the interviewer to not only hear your responses, but see *"who you are."* In addition, these types of screenings are a much better opportunity for you to sell yourself. Generally, face-to-face screening interviews are offered only to candidates within the local geographic region. Rarely is a company going to absorb the expense of bringing a candidate in from out of town if they have not first conducted a preliminary telephone screening.

You may also experience face-to-face screening interviews at job fairs. These types of interviews are usually quite brief as a result of the large number of potential applicants. In addition, many recruiters will conduct screenings to (1) determine if you are an appropriate candidate for a current search assignment, (2) determine if you might be a candidate for one of their client companies, although no active search is underway, (3) obtain additional information for future opportunities, or (4) get other candidate referrals from you.

HIRING INTERVIEWS

Hiring interviews are what most executive job search candidates consider the norm in interviewing. They are comprehensive interviews (generally after you have passed the screening interview) designed to allow you and the interviewer to explore your qualifications in much greater depth. These interviews are the first step in positioning yourself for a new career opportunity.

It is critical to remember that hiring interviews are two-way streets. Not only are you there to answer the interviewer's questions and sell your qualifications, you are also there with your own personal agenda. Is this the type of organization you want to work for? Does the company appear to be financially stable? What is the company's current market position? What are their key issues? What are their goals? Do you believe that you could deliver value to this organization? Would you be proud to work for them? Is it the *"right"* environment for you?

If your answers to these questions are negative, even though your interaction with the interviewer was positive, you may not want to take the opportunity any further. No need to waste your time or theirs. The only value in sustaining the relationship at this point is that (1) you believe that your issues can be addressed and resolved or (2) you believe that by continuing the interview process you may be able to obtain referrals and leads for other opportunities.

Hiring interviews generally take place in an office setting, but can be structured in one of six basic formats:

- One-On-One Interviews
- Serial Interviews

- Sequential Interviews
- Panel Interviews
- Candidate Group Interviews
- Out-of-the-Office Interviews

One-On-One Interviews

One-on-one, face-to-face interviews are the most common. While screening interviews are generally conducted by a human resource professional, hiring interviews are generally conducted by a decision maker—someone on either the senior or executive management team. Understand at this point that you will be asked very specific questions about your past employment experiences, responsibilities, accountabilities, projects, achievements, skills and qualifications. Although largely focusing on your professional experience, hiring interviews will also attempt to obtain relevant personal information about your management or leadership style, commitment, drive, energy, interests and personal character.

Serial Interviews

Serial interviews are similar to one-on-one interviews. The only difference is that you are scheduled, in advance, to meet with a number of individuals, one right after the other. No decision is made as to your qualifications until such time that all interviews have been completed and the interviewers compare their notes and observations, making their recommendations whether to eliminate you from consideration, invite you to continue in the interview process or make you an offer of employment.

These types of interviews can be exhausting. It is not unusual to start your day at 9 a.m. and not finish until 4 or 5 p.m. Your greatest challenge is to maintain your energy and drive throughout every session. Approach each interview as your first, highlighting your core qualifications and achievements, and communicating your value to the organization. Remember that each interviewer will have his/her own agenda so be sure to be responsive to the specific questions and issues at hand.

Sequential Interviews

Sequential interviews are now the norm for senior executive positions. They also are one-on-one interviews conducted over a period of time—days, weeks or even months. If, after completing hiring interview #1, you are still under consideration, you will be invited back for interview #2, then #3, etc., until everyone in the organization who wants or needs to interview you has, the company has determined that you are THE candidate and they make you an employment offer.

Sequential interviews are progressive, allowing you the opportunity to move forward in the hiring process, ask more intelligent questions as you delve further into the company and its operations, and provide each interviewer with more detail to substantiate your qualifications.

Sequential interviews tend to be with different people, again with their own agendas, questions, issues and concerns. Your challenge is to provide information, ask questions and sell the interviewer on your qualifications, value and candidacy. This is much easier to accomplish in sequential interviews as opposed to serial interviews. You are able to keep your enthusiasm high and your responses fresh because you have the time to prepare and energize between each interview.

Panel Interviews

These types of interviews can be the most intimidating. You can often feel as though it is you *"against"* all of them. Not only is the concept frightening, the physical environment and layout of the room can be threatening. You often feel pressured and under a great deal of stress. You've got one opportunity—and generally only one—to impress the entire group of panelists. Further, in this type of interview situation, it is often difficult for you to have much control. Although you may respond to one panelist's question and believe that he/she thought your answer to be quite appropriate, you are not aware of how the other panelists have interpreted your responses. Each person is there with his/her own agenda, making it difficult for you to respond to each individual person's concerns while meeting the concerns of all the other panelists.

The best strategy to succeed in this type of interview situation is to relax, be yourself, be confident in your abilities and work to clearly communicate your value. Realize that the chances are unlikely that you will meet every panelist's requirements 100%. It's okay. This is a group decision making process, generally not dependent upon the opinions or recommendations of just one individual. Be sure to make eye contact with each and every panelist throughout the interview session, demonstrating your interest, your response to their specific needs and your ability to function in a high-pressure, stressful environment.

Candidate Group Interviews

It is unlikely that in your search for an executive position you will ever be faced with a group interview situation—when a company interviews a number of candidates in one large group setting. These types of interviews are generally conducted for less experienced personnel when a company is attempting to evaluate the qualifications, interpersonal relations and communications skills of each candidate. How do they interact with their peers? What is their communications style? Are they easily intimidated? Do they take control? Are they polished in their presentation? By utilizing group interviewing strategies, companies are attempting to identify candidates that not only meet the qualifications of the position, but are confident and positive with a winning attitude.

Out-of-the-Office Interviews

Taking a prospective employee out to lunch or dinner is a great way to get to know them. The situation is more casual and the candidate is more relaxed. There is less structure and less stress. Companies will often use this tactic to get a glimpse into the *"real"* person—how they interact and communicate with others. These types of interviews are generally in the latter stages of the interview process, after you have already demonstrated that you have the basic qualifications for the position and after the company has already begun to consider you a top candidate. However, with the hectic pace so many of us keep today, mealtime interviews are increasing in frequency simply because of ease and efficient time management. No matter how casual the situation or the environment, always remember that out-of-the-office interviews are just that—interviews. Every word, gesture and mannerism will be closely observed and scrutinized.

TYPES OF INTERVIEW QUESTIONS

There are two basic types of interview questions, direct and indirect:

Direct Questions

- The most common type of interview questions.
- Specific questions requiring specific answers.
- Asked in a planned sequence and structure.
- Either closed or open-ended.
- Designed to explore specifics regarding your work experience, career objectives, special skills, educational credentials, technical proficiencies, strengths and weaknesses.

Example Questions:

"Are you PC literate?"

"What was your greatest achievement at IBM?"

"Are you willing to travel as the job may require?"

"How do you manage disgruntled, unmotivated staff?"

"How much was the largest budget you managed?"

"What was the largest number of staff you ever had reporting to you?"

Indirect Questions

- Less common than direct questions.
- Less structured than direct questions.
- Generally open-ended, providing you with the opportunity to elaborate on your skills, experiences, projects, achievements and career successes.

Example Questions:

"Tell me about yourself."

"Have you ever been involved in merger activities?"

"What are your long-term career goals?"

"Can you define your leadership style?"

"Are you an effective problem solver?"

"What motivates you?"

An effective executive job seeker is prepared for any type of interview, any type of question and any type of environment. Be sure that you thoroughly understand your product (YOU) and how to best present that product across a diversity of situations.

4

Overcoming
Obstacles to Opportunity

L earning to favorably present unfavorable situations
is one of the greatest challenges in the interview process. How can you explain why you were fired from
your last position without closing the door on your next
opportunity? How can you explain why you are currently
in a position several grades lower than that which you previously held? How will you counter the fact that the recommendation from your past supervisor is anything but flat-
tering? What do you tell someone when they ask why you
haven't worked for over a year now?

These questions, and others like them, present you with
unique interviewing challenges. You know that your goal
is to market your qualifications, performance and success.
You're in the interview to sell. But what can you do to overcome these difficult issues and still keep yourself in the
running, particularly when the competition is so fierce?

INTERVIEW CHALLENGE #1—YOU'VE BEEN FIRED!

Let us suppose that you were fired from your last position as Executive Vice President of Sales & Marketing for a
$225 million electronics and communications technology
manufacturer. You had been recruited two years previously
to plan and orchestrate the turnaround of the business. The
company was suffering from significant financial, customer

and market share losses, and was on the edge of bankruptcy. Your challenge was to restructure operations, introduce new products, expand market penetration, retrain staff and re-design core business processes. Further, there were major issues by and between the other executives—all family members. After two years, and with no notice, you were fired on a Monday morning. How can you positively present this?

"When I joined the company, I was challenged to lead the organization through a massive operating turn-around and market repositioning to restore profit-ability. The company had lost $25 million over the previous two years in addition to many of its major customers. Morale was low, product quality was poor and there was uncertainty as to whether the com-pany could survive. Through my efforts and those of my staff, we were able to effectuate a positive turn-around, halt losses and deliver the first profits in over three years. We redesigned major product lines, re-vitalized our image in the market, restored credibil-ity within the financial community and repositioned the company as a major competitor. Unfortunately, I was not able to resolve the in-fighting between the family members and their constant battle over money and control. As such, I often found myself in a posi-tion of mediating between the family and being forced to take sides on one issue after another. It was an extremely difficult situation. No matter my course of action and regardless of our strong finan-cial results, there was always a family member who felt as though I had betrayed him. I could never win. Then one morning, with no notice, two of the family members called me in, handed me my severance agreement and escorted me out the door. These two individuals had wanted to expand our sales into Eu-rope. I, and several others, had determined that it was premature at this point and made the decision to keep our sales domestic for at least one more year. Obviously, this decision did not sit well with the other two family members who, coincidentally, owned 60% of the company. I was immediately let go."

As discussed previously, this is a prime example of transitioning a negative into a positive. The candidate was honest (he was fired), but presented it in the most positive way possible with the emphasis on the success of the turn-around and revitalization of the company.

INTERVIEW CHALLENGE #2—YOU'RE OVERQUALIFIED FOR YOUR CURRENT JOB!

Consider the following scenario. After five years as CFO of an emerging biomedical technology company, the investors pulled out, the technology was acquired and the company was closed. With two kids in college and another a junior in high school, you needed a job immediately. Your savings had dwindled over the years and your wife's nursing job simply could not support the family. You were nervous and jumped at the first opportunity—a Controller position with a $500 million automotive products manufacturer. The position was 20 minutes from your home, and although you took a cut in pay, the ease and immediacy was well worth it. Now a year has passed and you are secure in your position, but you're bored and unchallenged. It's time for a change and time to get back to that top-level financial position. How do you explain all of this favorably without communicating the fact that you felt somewhat desperate at the time?

"I accepted the Controller position for one reason and one reason only—it was a unique opportunity to demonstrate the transferability of my skills from one industry to another. My entire career thus far had been in the biomedical, computer and telecommunications technology industries, and I was curious? How did other, non-technical industries operate? Were their financial needs so vastly different? Were their cost structures and budgeting processes unique? How much influence did industry specialization have upon the broader functions of strategic planning, change management and performance improvement? I wanted the chance to try my hand at something different from what I had been exposed to in the past.

"Well the last year has been quite a challenge. I have learned that, although the financial, accounting, budgeting, asset management and risk management processes are quite different, the underlying financial management strategies are quite similar. In turn, I have not only met my objectives, but exceeded them, introducing several novel financial and technical systems to more effectively manage our operations. Most notably, I decentralized budgeting and reduced operating costs $12 million annually, introduced sophisticated client/server technologies, and reallocated over $50 million in assets to support new product development.

"Now, however, I am ready for new challenges where I can again assume the level of financial and leadership responsibility which I have held in the past. I will look back upon my tenure here as a wonderful learning experience."

The success strategy in this instance is to bring the value of the experience to the forefront, pulling attention away from the lessened level of responsibility. Rather, focus on selling the unique aspects of the opportunity (e.g., industry diversification, responsibilities, new projects, new challenges) and its value in strengthening your executive skill set.

INTERVIEW CHALLENGE #3—YOUR RECOMMENDATIONS ARE POOR!

When you were hired by your current employer in 1989, you knew it was a great opportunity. Coming in as Regional Sales Manager, you earned six promotions in 10 years and advanced to your most recent position as Vice President of Sales for the North American market. Your career with the company was outstanding, except for your last position. A new EVP for Worldwide Sales was recruited in 1997 and, immediately upon his arrival, made massive organizational and staffing changes. Because of your tenure with the company, you were one of a select group of senior sales executives that was retained.

However, the situation became increasingly difficult as it was obvious that the new EVP was *"not in your corner."* Virtually overnight, your sales quotas and profit objectives were doubled. If it had been in the earlier years, you would have had no problem making the numbers. However, the market is quite mature now and growth at that pace is totally unrealistic. As such, for the first time since joining the company, you were not able to make your numbers and the EVP finally prevailed. On January 17, 1999, you were *"laid off"* in their words.

"In anticipation that you will be speaking with my most recent supervisor, I would like to make a few comments. I'm sure that Mr. Smith will tell you that I did not make my sales or profit objectives in 1998, that my performance was off track and that my commitment to the company was questionable. He will probably also mention that there was a severe lack of synergy between my style of sales management and his leadership objectives.

"I cannot argue any of these points. However, I can comment that prior to Mr. Smith's arrival with the company, I delivered a minimum of 120% of my quota for 10 consecutive years. Not only did my team achieve aggressive revenue and profit goals, I built what has now become known as the company's model sales organization. We were aggressive, we were successful and we were virtually unstoppable. Unfortunately, all of that changed in 1997 when new leadership arrived and sought to replace almost the entire executive sales management team. Because of my numbers and track record of performance, I was selected as one of only six senior sales executives offered the opportunity to remain with the company. I accepted the new challenges, restaffed my organization and attempted to move forward. However, the environment was not particularly supportive and there was an earnest desire to bring new talent in.

"I worked tirelessly over the next year to demonstrate my value to the new leadership team and my continued commitment to the organization. However, their goals included a "complete" restaffing. To ensure that would happen, the sales and profit quotas for each remaining executive were doubled while our budgets and resources were slashed. It was a no-win situation for everyone.

"I look back at the experience with no bitterness. An eleven-year career with such a prestigious company is an asset to anyone's career. It certainly has been to mine. I hope that you will take all of this information under advisement as you speak with Mr. Smith regarding my performance. I would also request that you contact Mr. Green, a long-time member of the executive team, who will be delighted to share information about my entire career with the company."

The strategy here is to favorably explain the situation, shift the onus away from yourself, and provide the name and contact information of someone within the organization who will *"sing your praises."*

INTERVIEW CHALLENGE #4—
YOU HAVEN'T WORKED FOR A YEAR!

This is every job seeker's worst nightmare—unemployment for an extended period of time. Let's suppose you were a veteran of IBM, with the company for more than 20 years, ever since college graduation. You advanced rapidly through a series of increasingly responsible manufacturing management positions to your final assignment directing all new manufacturing ventures and partnerships throughout Asia and Latin America. It was great. However, as the organization downsized, rightsized and reconfigured itself, you were caught in a massive layoff.

Your initial reaction was *"no problem."* With so many years of experience, you assumed your job search would be easy to manage. You were realistic, understanding that it would take some time, numerous contacts and an aggressive job search campaign. But you were optimistic.

Now, it is 13 months later and you're still in the market. How do you explain the situation without appearing undesirable?

"When I left IBM, I decided to take a short break after more than 20 years of steady employment. I wanted to spend some time with my family over the summer months, visit friends I had not seen in years and take a few computer courses to brush up on my hands-on skills. The time was invaluable to re-energize my mind, my heart and my soul.

"I then spent several months planning my job search, evaluating my career options and exploring the possibility of employment within upstate New York. At that time, I was not particularly interested in relocating my family. Rochester has been our home throughout my career. Unfortunately, as I'm sure you are aware, the Rochester market has been extremely hard hit as a result of the layoffs with IBM, Eastman

Kodak and several other large corporations. Employment opportunities are virtually non-existent at the level of position which I am seeking.

"Several months into my research and preparation it became obvious that I would have to consider relocation. Never one to forge ahead blindly, I spent a good deal of time investigating other geographic areas in the US to determine which markets were strongest, which markets offered the best public education opportunities, and which areas would be of interest both personally and professionally.

"I would have to say that I then began to conduct a serious job search, about seven to eight months after leaving IBM. As such, I have been actively seeking a new executive opportunity for only about five months now and have been fortunate to have been offered about 10-12 interviews. I am still interviewing with several of these companies; four positions were filled with internal candidates; two positions were downgraded; and two positions were filled by executives with more closely related industry experience. This opportunity with your organization appears to be an ideal match with my industry background and professional qualifications. Wouldn't you agree?"

With this type of response, you are changing your interviewer's perception of you from someone who has searched unsuccessfully for over a year to someone who has devoted the time, energy and resources necessary to plan and execute an appropriate search campaign. No, you have not been in the market for 13 months; only for five. No, you are not desperate, but rather looking for the *"right"* opportunity.

When responding to these difficult questions, it is imperative that you do not criticize your past employer, past supervisor or co-workers. You must make every attempt possible to positively position your responses without dishonesty or misrepresentation. Remember that your challenge is to sell your success, your contributions, your value and your track record of performance. It is okay to share the difficult situations and the not-so-pleasant facts. But be sure that you communicate in a positive manner and leave your interviewer with a favorable presentation. If you communicate a negative message about a past employer or supervisor, the result is a negative impression of you.

INTERVIEW CHALLENGE #5—IT's SOMEONE ELSE's AGENDA!

The one obstacle that you will never be able to overcome is someone else's agenda. There are so many factors beyond just you, your skills, qualifications, employment history and interview performance that will impact whether or not you are offered an opportunity. Each company and each hiring executive has his/her own agenda, needs and expectations. Some of these you can influence; others are totally out of your control and you may never even be aware of them.

Consider the following as just a few agenda issues that you cannot influence:

- Other candidates whose qualifications more closely match the company's needs.

- Other candidates whose industry experience more closely matches the company's needs.

- Other candidates whose network of contacts could be of more value to the company.

- The company's desire to hire a minority or woman, masking that behind the veil of interviewing every qualified applicant.

- Promotion of an internal candidate to the position.

- Elimination of the position through restructuring, downsizing, rightsizing or another corporate initiative.

- Company's poor financial performance and inability to commit to another executive salary.

- Company's takeover through a merger, acquisition, LBO or MBO.

- Recruitment and selection of a friend, past colleague or associate for the position.

Once you accept that there are things totally out of your control in the interview process, you will be better able to accept the loss and frustration you may feel when you are not offered an opportunity for which you thought yourself a *"perfect"* candidate. Sometimes it is best to just *"let it go."*

5
Winning Answers to
Tough Interview Questions

The following section contains 50 sample interview questions, many of which are asked in virtually every interview; others that are less frequently addressed. The answers that are provided should be used as strategic tools, ideas and concepts to help you formulate your own winning answers.

You Can Win!

To best exemplify how to respond to each of these questions, we have created a fictitious character—Edward J. Logan—a 50-year-old senior executive, currently employed as Executive Vice President with Broadcast Technology, Inc., an early stage venture that he joined in 1997. Ed began his career with a Fortune 500 company (X-Technolabs, Inc.), advanced rapidly through a series of increasingly responsible sales and marketing management positions, transitioning into senior management/general management six years ago. He was downsized in 1997 as part of a company-wide workforce reduction. It was then that he accepted the opportunity with his current employer, believing that the market potential for their technology was significant.

Ed has broad experience across all core functional disciplines including strategic planning, new venture planning, finance, technology development, field operations, sales, marketing and national account management. His experience also includes, but to a lesser degree, human resource affairs, purchasing, facilities management and community/corporate relations.

Ed has worked in start-up ventures, turnarounds and high-growth divisions in both US and international markets. He has been an active participant in due diligence reviews and financial negotiations for mergers, acquisitions, joint ventures and other strategic partnerships.

Ed believes that his negotiation, communication and interpersonal skills are what have propelled him throughout his career and been the driving force behind his success. Others have commented that Ed's greatest value is his consistent ability to deliver positive financial results, despite market conditions, regulatory challenges and competitive forces. Ed has taken this comment and integrated it into his search strategy, believing that although the humanistic characteristics of a strong business leader are vital, the bottom-line financial results will catch someone's attention.

To better understand the following responses, consider that Ed is currently interviewing for a position as the President of The Technology Team, Inc. (hereinafter referred to as TTT), a $75 million telecommunications company servicing the Northern California market. The company needs fresh ideas, a new market vision and renewed energy to continue its growth and expansion throughout the national market.

Tell me about yourself.

This question is one of the classics and there are two vastly differing schools of thought on how to best respond. Tradition tells us that what someone is asking you for is a brief summation of your career. As succinctly as possible, lead your interviewer through your career history with a brief mention of some of your most notable achievements.

Ed would say, "I began my career with X-Technolabs in 1974, was selected for the executive leadership development program after just two years, and earned eight other promotions during my tenure. My earliest experiences were in field marketing, sales and regional management. In each position, I delivered strong revenue results. I was then promoted to the senior management team of a troubled business unit, working with two other executives to facilitate its turnaround. Once profitable, I left that unit and spent the next three years introducing internal change and organizational development programs throughout the corporation. The next several years were devoted to developing new ventures as our industry exploded. My final assignment was a General Manager of a $150 million business unit where not only did I deliver a 25% improvement in bottom-line profitability, I helped to position the company as the #1 market leader in the industry.

"Currently, I am employed as the Executive Vice President with Broadcast Technology. I joined the company in 1997 after a careful review of their technology, proposed marketing strategy and high level of technical talent. My responsibilities are largely devoted to providing strategic direction for both technology development and market launch, planned for mid-1999. To date, my team and I have closed over $45 million in sales prior to full product roll-out. In addition, I have been an active leader in developing the company's manufacturing and production processes, working with our plant management team to create a best-in-class organization."

More modern thought has changed the strategy for answering this question. Instead of giving a career history that virtually reiterates what is already on your resume and will be the foundation for the remainder of the interview, use this question wisely and to your advantage. Briefly, and with powerful words, summarize *"who you are today"* and the value you bring to that organization. Your answer can incorporate results and experiences from your past, but should not simply repeat what is on the resume. Focus on the *"professional"* you with some *"personal"* mixed in as appropriate.

If Ed were to answer the *"Tell me about yourself"* question using this strategic approach, he would state,

"I am a well-qualified, senior-level management executive who has met the unique challenges of start-up, turnaround and high-growth companies. Never working in what one would consider a status quo organization, I have continually been challenged to deliver results that required strong creative, strategic and tactical leadership. Most significantly, in each and every one of these situations, I have delivered measurable financial improvements in revenue, market share, cost and bottom-line profitability.

"A few specific examples that best exemplify my performance include my current leadership of an early stage technology venture for which I have generated $45 million in new revenues within one year. In my previous position as the General Manager of the Partners in Technology Division of X-Technolabs, my team and I not only improved profitability 25% but also positioned the company as #1 in the national market. Earlier career achievements were equally notable during my tenure in sales, marketing, turnarounds and new venture development.

"In summary, I consider myself a consummate management professional, confident in my ability to tackle virtually any challenge by assembling the right personnel, identifying the appropriate markets and building product recognition despite competition. Of paramount importance to my success has been my ability to build relationships throughout all levels of an organization, defining common goals, implementing incentives and challenging my workforce to deliver their best."

With the above answer, you get a much clearer sense of Ed's value, energy and results. The presentation is sharper, more aggressive and on the *"executive"* level.

Now, onto Ed's answers to the remainder of the interview questions.

How long have you been looking for a new position?

"I launched my search several months ago, but very quietly and confidentially. Since then, I have been on about 10 interviews, making it to the final group in all but three. In fact, I was offered an opportunity with another emerging technology company but was extremely concerned about their long-term market potential so I declined the opportunity.

"Because I am currently employed, and secure in my position for the immediate future, I do not feel the need to jump into another opportunity. Unless, of course, the opportunity is the 'right' one for me and for the company."

Why are you considering leaving your current position (applicable only if employed)?

"Although I still believe that Broadcast Technology has great technological innovation and tremendous market potential, the investor group backing the company has decided to not invest any further funds in R&D or market development. As such, although the company has experienced strong growth over the past year, I anticipate the growth curve will ebb. As with any emerging venture, financial backing is critical to long-term development. Considering the circumstances, I have determined that it is perhaps best if I resign my position and look for opportunities elsewhere.

"Let me just mention that neither the investor group nor the other members of the executive team are aware of my decision. I prefer to keep my search confidential until such time as I have received an offer. I am sure that you understand and appreciate my situation."

What did you wish to accomplish in your current job but were unable to do? Why?

"What I was unable to do in my current position was negotiate for additional funding from our investor group. The company is owned by a small venture capital firm which invests only in emerging technology companies. As a result of their narrow investment focus and the tremendous volatility within virtually all technology industries, they have suffered significant financial losses over the past year. Although Broadcast Technology delivered strong revenue results, the investors determined that they were not willing to increase our funding, no matter the long-term potential. The President of the company has not given up hope and is currently negotiating with two other investor groups who may have a potential interest. However, the situation is now much too uncertain for me to remain."

Why did you leave your last postion?

"I left my position with X-Technolabs after 23 years because the company was no longer thriving. During my tenure we had experienced a long period of phenomenal growth in all of our core business units. The environment was dynamic and the results unprecedented in the industry. Unfortunately, in the early and mid 1990's, as the industry experienced tremendous competition, we found ourselves floundering. Our technologies were becoming outdated, many of our international joint ventures were experiencing financial difficulties, and our cash situation was at its worst ever. At that point the company felt the need to undergo massive internal change and reorganization. Over 35% of the entire workforce was downsized, including me and more than 35 other senior managers and executives. Although I was sad to leave the company after so many years, the change afforded me the opportunity to again join a high-growth venture. I look back at my years with X-Technolabs with tremendous pride and personal satisfaction."

What will your current supervisor say about your performance (or most recent past supervisor)?

"Currently I report to the President of Broadcast Technology who is not aware of my decision to seek a new career opportunity. As such, I would ask you not to contact him at this point in time. Of course, if we come to a mutual agreement, I know that you will eventually want to speak with him.

"What will he say about me? I believe that John will comment on my ability to provide vision and then translate that vision into specific action plans. He will tell you that one of my greatest contributions to the company has been my ability to build consensus and create a team-based environment. He will also mention the strength of my communication and negotiation skills, my ability to accurately assess the potential of proposed new ventures, and my involvement in controlling operating costs during a period of growth and expansion. Perhaps most significantly, he will substantiate the fact that my contributions were the catalyst for our strong revenue growth this past year."

What will your colleagues say about you?

"My colleagues will tell you that I know what I am doing, that I am able to quickly grasp control of a situation, make tough decisions and move forward."

How would your subordinates describe you?

"I believe that the majority of individuals who have worked for me will tell you that I am honest, fair and above board. I don't believe that there should be any secrets (other than proprietary financial, market, product and/or technology information). As such, I think that my teams have felt they each contributed and that their efforts were noticed and appreciated. I believe that everyone wants to feel as though they are valued.

"My employees will also tell you that I am a good listener. I value their opinions and am willing to take the time to hear what they have to say.

"Lastly, I think they will say that they had to work hard for me. I expect a lot from them, but am willing to give a lot in return."

What did your most recent performance appraisal say about the quality of your performance?

"My last performance review focused primarily on the financial results my team and I were able to deliver. As you are now aware, we increased revenues by $45 million within that year, improved our market share ratings and initiated development of our next generation technology.

"My review commented on the value of my leadership competencies, my success in providing a renewed corporate vision and my performance in pulling the team together to deliver such results. Additional comments reflected my strong communication skills, interpersonal relations skills, and ability to evaluate proposed new ventures and accurately forecast their potential.

"Broadcast Technology ranks executive performance on a scale of 1-5 with 5 being outstanding. I received a rating of 5 on 27 of the 30 criteria; the remaining 3 were rated as 4."

Have you ever been fired or resigned from a position?

"Fortunately, I have not. But as we have discussed, I am considering resignation from my current position due to lack of investor funding to support continued growth, technology development and international expansion."

What is the greatest value you bring to this organization?

"The greatest value I bring to TTT is my ability to deliver positive financial results. Most relevant to your organization has been my success in accelerating growth through new product development, new market development, sales training and expansion into alternate distribution channels. As General Manager of X-Technolabs, I delivered 25% revenue growth within an intensely competitive market, improved our market share by 16% and increased our national account base by more than 40%. More recently, with Broadcast Technology, I have provided the strategy and operating leadership that has increased our revenues by more than 100% in less than one year. Second year projections forecast an additional 75% growth in the US market with initial penetration into Latin American and European markets."

Note that Ed is using specific examples of his past job responsibilities to highlight his achievements as they directly relate to the needs of the company. In just five quick sentences, he was able to communicate action, results, success and value.

What are your immediate, 5-year and 10-year goals—personally and professionally?

"My current goals are focused on obtaining a new senior executive opportunity within the technology industry. It is where I can be of most value and deliver the strongest results. The ideal position would entail a vast array of responsibilities, including P&L, strategic planning, new venture development, finance and budgeting, sales, marketing and organizational development. From what I have learned about your company and your current search, I believe that this may be just the right opportunity for us both.

"My goals for the next 5-10 years would include continued progression to executive positions of even greater financial, marketing, strategic and operating responsibility. A company such as this would provide just the right environment to increase my leadership responsibilities as you continue to penetrate new markets, build new technologies and expand your customer base. I believe that I can provide the energy, strategy and tactical operating leadership critical to your profitable growth."

Define your leadership and management style?

"My leadership style is rooted in my belief that no organization is stronger than its workforce. To that end, I have worked tirelessly throughout my career to create working environments that encourage individual development, performance and reward. If it were not for the commitment and effort of my staff, many of the successes I have achieved would never have been possible. Employees are the backbone of any successful organization. They are what keep it moving forward internally and what earns our reputation externally.

"Creating team-based environments is one of my greatest strengths. I do not believe in the traditional hierarchy of 'them and us,' realizing that each individual employee wants to believe that his/her contributions are core to the success of the company. As such, I have led numerous internal change and organizational development initiatives, all of which were focused on creating a proactive, team-based organization working collaboratively to achieve our goals, meet our challenges and realize our vision.

"As you take all of this into consideration, it is also important to remember that someone has to be the team leader, the key decision maker and the impetus driving the organization forward. Although I am always dedicated to my workforce and strive to make them feel a part of our success, I do also appreciate that my role as team leader is equally significant. If the team does not have a primary voice, there is no direction. I have always been that voice, guiding each organization to success while nurturing and energizing the workforce."

Define your decision making style?

"The word proactive perhaps best describes my decision making style. Never daunted by challenge, I approach each business decision much like I would a puzzle, looking at each individual piece and then integrating them into one whole to see the entire picture.

"I believe that no decision relies just on one piece of information. The internal and external factors influencing a company are much too complex. Effective decision making requires a thoughtful process to clearly and accurately analyze all factors which not only affect the decision today, but the long-term impact throughout the company.

"I also believe that it is vital to encourage the participation and input of others within the organization. Certain decisions may be straightforward; others require greater contemplation during which the opinions and recommendations of my staffs and management teams have been essential."

Define your success in problem solving?

"Let me begin by stating that I attempt to view problems not as problems but as challenges and opportunities for positive change. With that in mind, let me discuss my tenure as one of three senior executives leading X-Technolabs' core technology division through a dramatic turnaround, revitalization and return to profitability.

"For more than 15 years, the division had operated profitably, met its goals, launched revolutionary new technology and established itself as a market leader. More recently, it had faced escalating operating costs, a volatile marketplace and instability within the workforce. Budgets were out of control, managers were not performing to plan and financial results had plummeted.

"Before making any decisions as to what course of action to take, I created a structured process to investigate the situation. I began with a comprehensive review of the organization, working to identify the specific issues that had so negatively impacted the organization. This required extensive research and communication with individuals throughout the entire organization, an in depth analysis of financial results, interactions with customers, communications with vendors and a host of other research-based efforts. Once I had obtained the preliminary data, my management team and I spent weeks analyzing, extrapolating and interpreting the information, providing us with a clear picture of the factors negatively impacting performance.

"Once the other executives and I understood the situation, we were able to devise the strategies, introduce the business processes and lead the internal change initiatives to regain control and reenergize operations. In summary, we not only achieved our turnaround objectives but exceeded them. Costs were cut by as much as 32% in the production area, sales productivity increased 28%, market share reached an all time high and profitability was restored within the first year.

"Based upon my success in uncovering the underlying issues impacting performance, I then spent the next several years working as an executive trouble-shooter throughout numerous divisions, business units, joint ventures and operations within X-Technolabs. Using the formula I had developed, I was able to quickly go into each organization, identify the core issues, implement new strategies, revitalize operations and restore performance. I am particularly proud of my success in this role."

Tell me about your communication skills?

"Let me use this opportunity to highlight my communication skills as they relate to external corporate affairs with our customers, bankers, vendors and financiers.

"Maintaining relationships with customers was critical to both Broadcast Technology and X-Technolabs, just as it is to TTT. We are in a customer-driven industry where our name, our image and our market perception are vital to our performance. Appreciating the tremendous influence our customers have, I have always made it a point to maintain an active communication channel throughout the customer base. This has included direct presentations and negotiations with national and other large accounts, as well as a quarterly newsletter I developed that is distributed to all customers throughout both US and international markets. My sales and marketing management teams know that I am readily available to support their efforts, resolve problems and provide whatever type of customer support or communication may be necessary to ensure quality service and retention.

"In relation to my involvement in communicating with the banking community, I have always played an active role in establishing commercial banking, credit and lending relationships. Working with the CFO's of both companies, I participated in defining our immediate and long-term cash requirements, negotiating corporate lines of credit and introducing strategic cash management tools. My value in these communications has not only been my knowledge of the business, the industry and the market, but my strength in building relationships based on trust and integrity.

"Vendors have been another audience with whom I have communicated, primarily related to price, performance and quality. Most significantly, I assisted X-Technolabs' Manufacturing Manager in developing a process to enhance vendor communications, eliminate inaccuracies, and assure that all parties were aware of the needs and expectations of the other. These types of efforts were particularly critical in supporting our new ventures and turnaround efforts.

"In relation to our financiers, in my current position I communicate regularly with the venture capital firm funding our operations. Primarily this has included presentations regarding the company's financial status and formal requests for additional funding. The latter has been quite similar to what is commonly referred to as road show presentations, outlining our current operations, use of funds and projected results. Again, my ability to communicate openly and honestly has been a catalyst in nurturing these relationships."

Tell me about your negotiation skills?

"To best exemplify my negotiating skills let me tell you about a new venture I developed while working for X-Technolabs.

"In 1989, I realized that the opportunity for expansion into European markets was emerging. To capitalize upon that opportunity, I researched potential joint venture partners in the UK, France, Germany and Spain. After months of investigation and preliminary discussions, I determined that the most advantageous opportunity would be a co-marketing agreement with a French-based technology company.

"The negotiations for this venture were intense. X-Technolabs had its objectives, and while the French company was also motivated by the potential financial rewards of this venture, they had their own priorities. To achieve consensus, I assembled the three top decision makers from each organization for an entire week of negotiations. During this time, we addressed each and every issue impacting our agreement, redefined our strategy, realigned our field coverage and outlined new areas of responsibility. All financial considerations were closely addressed until we reached agreement. On day four, the deal was closed. We then spent day five touring local sites and getting to know each other better. Over the first two years the partnership generated $180 million in revenues, well beyond the best of anyone's expectations."

Are you PC literate?

"Yes, I have excellent PC skills and consider myself proficient with Word, Excel and PowerPoint. Of course, I am not a programmer or systems analyst, but I have worked closely with senior-level IT staff throughout my career to translate our business needs into technology applications. Let me also mention that I am Internet savvy and a great advocate of email. What a time saver it has become."

What are the greatest contributors to your success?

"As I have previously mentioned, I believe that the most vital contributors to my personal success are my communication, interpersonal relations, mentoring, coaching and team building skills. Earlier in our discussion, I outlined my commitment to developing and nurturing my workforce, believing that they are the foundation for any company's success. Of course the vision, energy and leadership style of the executive team is just as critical. However, without the support of each and every employee to achieving that vision and meeting organizational goals, there would be no success. It is through their daily efforts and contributions that performance, financial, operating and strategic objectives are met, if not exceeded.

"I learned quite early in my career that if I was successful in building top-performing teams, not only did we achieve our objectives, but our perception in the marketplace would be strong. As such, I have devoted my energies to creating organizations with open channels of communication across all levels and have been successful in integrating mentoring, employee development and team building programs. The results of these efforts are clearly supported when you review the financial performance of each organization under my leadership."

How do you deal with stressful situations?

"I take a step back and take a deep breath! In fact, I sometimes think that I am the poster child for stressful situations—aggressive start-up ventures, high-growth companies, operating unit turnarounds and other performance-driven situations. Each of these involved different stresses, but the ultimate goal for each was improved revenue and profit performance. And yes, I felt the stress to perform—stress from the Board of Directors, shareholders, executive management teams and operating management teams. Schedules were often demanding, budgets were tight and our goals were aggressive.

"However, stress is only as intense as you allow it to be. Over the years I've learned to look at these situations objectively and not allow myself to get caught up in the tension and anxiety. It has been critical, that as the leader of these organizations, I am able to maintain my composure, make good decisions and continue to move forward. To accomplish this requires effective skills not only in stress management, but in problem solving, decision making, consensus building and organizational leadership."

What is the #1 achievement of your career?

"My most notable achievement occurred early on in my career as Regional Sales & Marketing Manager for X-Technolabs' Mid-Atlantic region. During my 2-year tenure in this position, I was able to increase regional revenues by more than 100%, captured over 500 new corporate accounts, achieved dominant market positioning and virtually eliminated competitive threats.

"Now, when you look at my more recent achievements you may think that they have been grander. And perhaps they have. However, this early success gave me the confidence in myself, my skills and my performance that has propelled my career thereafter. I would have to say that, on a personal note, this achievement was the most vital."

What are the top 5 contributions you have made during your career?

"We have probably already covered some of this information in our earlier discussion, so I will briefly highlight what I consider to be my most valuable contributions and achievements.

- $45 million revenue growth in one year for Broadcast Technology.

- Successful turnaround and return to profitability of X-Technolabs' core operating division.

- Negotiation and development of 8 joint ventures in the US, Europe and Latin America on behalf of X-Technolabs, a step that was vital in expanding the company's presence throughout both US and international markets.

- Road show presentations that raised over $200 million in venture capital and institutional funds to finance development of X-Technolabs' next generation technology.

- Strong and steady revenue, market share and profit improvements I delivered early in my field sales and marketing management career."

What are your greatest strengths?

"My strengths are reflected by strong financial results and my ability to build, energize, develop and lead top-performing teams. It's the money and the people."

What are your weaknesses?

"I believe my greatest weakness is impatience, wanting results today, not six months down the road. When I accept a new assignment, I am energized and immediately ready to move forward. However, over the years, I have learned to temper this enthusiasm with the realization that progress takes time, money, energy and dedication. Success does not come overnight.

"I might also comment that over time I have learned to place reasonable expectations on my staff. Early in my career, I believed that everyone should work 70 hours a week and make the job their life. However, I can now appreciate the fact that although my employees work hard and give a lot of themselves, they are not 'married' to their jobs. They do have lives beyond work and I must respect that. Don't worry though; I still expect them to give 110% everyday."

What motivates you to perform and excel?

"Challenge has always been my #1 motivator. When I look back at my college years, I can see it then. On the track team for four years, each year I set a goal for myself to improve my time. And each year I exceeded the goal because I was internally motivated and self-challenged to deliver. That part of my personality continues to thrive today and is evidenced by my success in leading new technology ventures through growth, expansion, internal change and performance improvement. The personal pride I feel when I have met my goals is enormous and will continue to drive my performance for the rest of my life."

Do you consider yourself a leader or a follower?

"Definitely a leader, but a participative leader. I thrive on the challenges of leading organizations and people, but also know that I do not have all the answers. As such, I have always maintained a cooperative working environment, valuing the ideas, recommendations and contributions of others—my management teams, my professional staffs and my hourly personnel. Ultimately, however, one person has to make the decisions and be accountable. I have worked to place myself in that leadership position since early in my career, and even as far back as high school and college. I was class president in my junior and senior years at the University of Missouri, was team captain of both my high school and college golf teams, and was active in leading various community sponsored events."

Are you a risk taker?

"I am a calculated risk taker. Before moving forward on any project, I attempt to collect as much information as possible to ensure that my decisions are based on fact and evidence, and not gut reaction. However, I also realize that those who are not aggressive in moving forward often do not win. I believe that a certain risk level is necessary for any executive to effectively lead a high-growth, high-performance organization."

How do you determine or evaluate success?

"I believe that success can be measured in two distinct ways: First, by bottom-line financial results and second, by personal pride and satisfaction."

What is the worst mistake you ever made on the job and how did you remedy the situation?

"The single worst mistake of my career was in 1984 when, as Regional Sales Manager, I ordered the production of 5000 printed circuit boards for a new customer. Doesn't sound so bad does it? However, I ordered production prior to the client's signature on the contract. I was young and the client assured me that he wanted the product. I was anxious to please, so I moved forward. Four days later, the client informed me that he had found a better price and was not interested in my products any longer. Even after all of these years, I can still remember how I felt that day. The wind had been knocked out of my sails. I went home devastated.

"Two days later I was renewed. I knew that I had 5000 PCB's to sell immediately and I set out to find a new customer. Over the next three weeks, I knocked on more doors than I had ever done, negotiated aggressive incentive programs with my distributors and never gave up. I found a new buyer who not only purchased the 5000, but ordered an additional 10,000 over the next year.

"Needless to say, I have never again launched production until the contract has been signed."

What have you learned from your mistakes?

"Perhaps the greatest lesson I have learned is accountability. If I make a mistake, I must assume responsibility. As I have progressed throughout my career to positions of significant decision making authority, I've taken the glory and the pats on the back. But I have also learned to take responsibility when results have not been what we anticipated or mistakes have been costly. As the business leader, no matter who in my organization makes a decision, I must ultimately accept the responsibility."

If you could change something about your life, what would it be and why?

"If we're talking on a professional level, I would have returned to college and earned my MBA degree. Although I do not believe it would make me any more qualified than I am now, the classroom is always a dynamic environment from which we can all glean new information, concepts, strategies and tools."

What are your views on continuing education? For yourself? For your employees?

"Continuing education is vital, particularly in an industry such as ours that is so rapidly evolving. To that end, I have made a point of devoting time and energy to continuing my education. This includes attendance at more than 200 hours of courses over the past 10 years, including graduation from

Harvard's Executive MBA Program and attendance at the Center for Creative Leadership. Much of my continuing education has focused on further developing my managerial, leadership, communication, negotiation and strategic planning skills. In addition, I have taken several short courses to improve my hands-on PC skills.

"In reference to my employees, I also consider continuing education vital to both their personal and professional development. I actively encourage their enrollment in training programs and college courses and, when appropriate, am more than willing to absorb the training costs. Further, I have justified development of numerous in-house training programs to provide the entire workforce with the opportunity for skills development. The results of these efforts have been a more motivated, more qualified and more committed workforce who also understands and appreciates the value of continuing education to their current positions and long-term career goals."

Who was your most valuable mentor and why?

"The single greatest influence in my career was a gentleman named Ted Smith. He was my first supervisor when I joined X-Technolabs. As Ted was promoted, so was I, giving us the opportunity to work together for more than five years.

"Ted taught me and nurtured me, adding to my responsibilities as I was ready, giving me new challenges to spark my performance, and always being available to support, guide and mentor me. I believe that Ted's guidance accelerated the pace of my career development and growth. The valuable lessons he taught will be with me throughout my career and my life."

When you are hiring, what do you look for as the most important attribute in a candidate?

"By far, the single most important characteristic of any individual's success is attitude. Although I firmly believe that an individual must have the basic skills to perform the function, attitude is vital. An individual must want the position, have a positive attitude, be willing to learn and have strong interpersonal skills. If someone has the basic qualifications, I can teach the job and fine tune his/her skills. However, I cannot change attitude."

Have you ever had a supervisor you did not get along with and how did you manage the relationship?

"Early in my career, I worked for a gentleman who had been with the company for over 30 years. As Director of Field Sales, he was fully accountable for the profitable performance of the entire sales organization. I was one of his regional managers, responsible for the Midwest territory, including both commercial and government accounts. The first day we met it was evident that there would be conflict. I was eager to accelerate growth within my region, full of new ideas and energy, and ready to tackle the world. My manager, on the other hand, was extremely cautious, content with the status quo and not anxious to make waves during his last two years with the company. Every time I approached him with a new concept or new marketing strategy, he listened but was quite resistant to change. As hard as I pushed to launch some of my ideas, he stood firm.

"Fortunately, both of us realized that we would be working together for two years and that we must find some common ground. At my urging, he and I agreed to an informal meeting outside of the office where we would both be comfortable in discussing our situation. We spent hours together that night, learned a great deal about each other and did find our common ground. I appreciated his situation; he learned to appreciate my talent and drive. Together, over the next two years, we further developed my region, realized a 32% increase in sales revenues and were both commended by the executive team for our performance.

"This was a most valuable lesson, teaching me that in virtually any circumstance, individuals can find common ground upon which to build."

Have you ever had to fire someone for poor performance? How did you manage the situation?

"When I assumed leadership responsibility for the turnaround of X-Technolabs' core operating division, I was faced with a difficult situation. The individual who was responsible for the entire production planning, scheduling and materials management function had not been performing to plan. His previous manager had discussed this with him on numerous occasions and clearly documented all their discussions. New plans had been devised and new processes had been developed, but nothing was ever implemented. Further, it was clearly evident that his mismanagement of these functions had a negative impact throughout the entire organization, was a primary cause for budget excesses and had been the leading contributor to poor product quality.

"I took immediate action, informing this individual that if his performance did not measurably improve over the next 30 days, he would be let go. Each week, for the following four weeks, I met with him to discuss his progress and provide my support. Still no effort and no results. Therefore, I did terminate his employment after 30 days and promoted an individual from within to assume his position. Subsequently, over the next six months, our budgets were back in line, quality was improved by better than 85% and we were well on our way to recovery.

"This experience was difficult for me. In the past, if I had individuals who were not meeting expectations, I was always able to work with them to enhance their performance. This particular individual was not willing to make any changes, accept constructive criticism or work with other members of the team. I had no alternative."

What are you looking for in a new opportunity?

"Challenge and the opportunity to make a difference. One thing that has always distinguished my career has been the opportunity to participate in a diversity of functions, projects, new ventures and turn-arounds. Each position has had its own set of challenges to be met, ranging from negotiating strategic alliances and joint ventures to redesigning manufacturing processes and cost structures, and everything in between. This is what has been my motivator—the chance to make a difference.

"It is a similar type of opportunity that I am currently seeking. I know myself well enough to know that I would not be content with the status quo. I want the chance to help a company grow and prosper. And, I would be proud to have the opportunity to work with you in achieving just that for TTT."

How would you describe your ideal position?

"I have probably described my ideal position in what I have just told you. Let me also mention, however, that I am seeking a position that will afford me a great deal of responsibility and decision making authority. I am accustomed to that level of accountability and look forward to continuing as one of several top executives of an organization. I would also anticipate having either direct and/or joint profit and loss responsibility.

"I want to be at the helm of an organization and be one of the individuals accountable for its growth and strong financial performance. The personal satisfaction I derive is what continues to move my professional career forward."

What other positions are you interviewing for?

"Currently, I am actively interviewing for two very different positions—one as General Manager of a small, yet well-established and financially-solid telecommunications manufacturing firm. I have interviewed twice with this company and am scheduled for a third interview in two weeks.

"The other position I am actively interviewing for is as Executive Vice President of Sales & Marketing for a Fortune 100 technology company. I had a brief conversation with the COO of the company last week and he was quite interested in my experience in new venture development. Yesterday, I spoke with his secretary to coordinate my travel arrangements and will be meeting with him early next month.

"Both positions require an experienced senior executive capable of defining a new strategic direction, assembling the resources and building market presence to drive revenue growth. In fact, virtually all the positions I have investigated—whether general management or executive-level sales management—have focused on companies seeking to grow and expand either in US and/or international markets."

What criteria are you using to evaluate the different companies you are interviewing with?

"I would have to say that the primary criterion is the company's opportunity—its products, technologies and market potential. I want to align myself with an organization that is moving forward, growing and expanding. Of course, the financial stability of the organization is also quite important, but often there are inherent risks in taking advantage of new business opportunities.

"I would be amiss if I didn't also mention compensation. Of course, I am looking for an opportunity where my compensation—whether it be salary, bonus, incentive and/or equity—is commensurate with the energy, drive and results I will deliver. Each of us wants to be acknowledged for our efforts and our contributions."

Is job security a prime consideration for you?

This is a particularly tricky question to answer. Consider the fact that companies want to hire individuals who are committed to the organization, its growth and its success. However, you must counterbalance that with the undeniable fact that today's corporate employment market is volatile and ever changing. The long-term security once offered by large corporations has, to a large degree, disappeared over the past decade. Companies don't want to "marry" you; they want you to come in, fill an immediate need and remain as long as the opportunity exists—a year, three years or 10. Situations change and you must be flexible. Ed would respond with,

"Of course, job security is a consideration. But perhaps more important is the opportunity and the challenge that it offers. I know that no company can assure an executive of a long tenure in an employment market that is so volatile. Technologies are changing rapidly and companies must respond to this change. As such, a company's needs often change over time. Would I like to think that I might remain with TTT for 5 years, 10 years or more? Of course. However, I am realistic in my expectations and know that things can suddenly and unexpectedly change after just a few years. I have accepted that as part of my executive career and am willing to take whatever risks are associated with opportunity for success and reward."

How long do you expect to stay with our company?

"I would hope that this opportunity with TTT would be long-term as the company continues to grow and expand. To be perfectly honest, I am not particularly interested in accepting an opportunity that is only anticipated to last for a year or two. I am hoping to find an opportunity where I can be of value and contribute for years and years to come. Obviously, however, this will depend not only upon my personal success, but the success of the organization."

Suppose we were to offer you the position of President of TTT. If you could have only two other executives working with you to build this company, what would those individuals be responsible for and why?

"I would have a Chief Financial Officer and a Human Resource Executive. I believe that the former is critical to any corporation. In order for me to perform my functions as the President or CEO of an organization, I need to know the financial facts and anticipated outcomes. The information and knowledge that the CFO provides is vital in plotting the best course of action.

"Equally essential is the Director of HR. Although a great part of my career has been invested in developing my workforce, mentoring them, coaching them and energizing them, I am not an HR Executive. I do not administer benefits and compensation; I do not develop HR information systems, and I have not been responsible for HR regulatory affairs. However, these functions are essential and require the skills of a specialist.

"If you combine the expertise of these two individuals with my strong general management, leadership, marketing and organizational development skills, you would indeed have a winning executive team at TTT."

What will you bring to this position that another candidate will not?

"Not familiar with the other candidates that you are interviewing for this position, I would comment that the four greatest assets I bring to TTT are:

- My ability to see the entire picture and how each functional discipline impacts the whole organization.

- My ability to consistently, and despite market conditions, deliver strong financial results.

- My energy, drive and dedication.

- My in depth knowledge of, and experience in, the industry. With over 20 years of experience, I know the players, the markets and the technologies. This information and these contacts will inevitably provide TTT with a strong competitive advantage."

Are you willing to travel? How often?

"Yes, I am more than willing to travel as may be required. Throughout my career, I have been in a position where travel was a necessary part of the job.

This has included travel to customer sites, company operating locations, and new ventures in both the US and abroad.

"In the past, I have traveled as much as 35% of my time. More recently, it has been approximately 15%. That percentage of travel is acceptable. However, I do understand that there may be times when my travel schedule would be more demanding as new ventures evolve, new markets are penetrated and new partners are brought aboard."

What is your expectation for number of hours to be worked each week?

"I would anticipate, at least initially, that I would be working a minimum of 70 hours per week. Perhaps more. None of my positions over the past 10 years have required less than an average of 55 hours per week; sometimes as much as 80+ hours if we were working on a particularly time sensitive project or new initiative. I hope that I have already displayed my willingness to work hard, my initiative and my commitment. That commitment extends to include whatever time may be necessary to plot our course, develop our business and achieve the Board's financial objectives. I am not afraid of hard work and not intimidated by long hours. Success requires effort and perseverance."

Why are you interested in our company?

When this question is posed, you had better know the answer! There are many resources available to find information about the company you will be interviewing with. Call for an annual report, search the Internet, visit your local library or make some phone calls. People want to hire people that know about them, not just have simply heard about them. Be sure that you are well prepared, have learned about the history of the company, its current operations, products, services and/or technologies. An educated job seeker is always a winner!

> Ed would respond with, "I am well aware of the success of TTT. I have always made it a point of knowing my competition, the major players in the industry and the early stage ventures that are poised to make a real impact—just like TTT.

> "My interest in TTT is for precisely that reason. Aware of the quality of your technology and the widespread impact it has already had in the industry, I know that the company will continue to grow, expand and prosper. And I want to work for a winner. In researching TTT, I have also learned that your goals include international expansion into both the Latin American and European markets, both of which I have had direct experience with. Further, I am acquainted with several of the members of your Board of Directors, individuals I worked with and/or negotiated with during my career with X-Technolabs.

> "TTT is definitely poised for dramatic growth and I am confident in my abilities to lead the organization to achieve your current goals and long-term objectives."

What type of person would you hire for this position?

> "If the hiring decision was mine, I would outline the following characteristics for the 'ideal' hire. They would include the ability to see the big picture, ability to deliver strong financial results, energy and drive, and industry knowledge."

Obviously, you are telling your interviewer that you would hire someone with precisely your qualifications without being quite so blatant with your statement. If you refer to the question that addressed *'What you would bring to this position that another candidate would not?',* you will note that Ed's answer to this question directly mirrors his own strengths, attributes and qualifications.

Why should we hire you?

This is a critical question that allows you to succinctly and aggressively summarize your qualifications. Very often it will be asked as one of the last questions in an interview. If it is not asked by the end of the interview, it is your responsibility to introduce the topic. If the interview is coming to a close, you should end your presentation with, *"Let me tell you why you should offer me this opportunity."* Then proceed with your answer which should summarize your core qualifications and experience as they pertain directly that position.

Ed ends his interview with, "You should offer me this opportunity because I am extremely well-qualified and believe that I have demonstrated to you my ability to deliver financial results within competitive new ventures and high-growth companies. Further, I have an excellent knowledge of, and network in, the technology industry, relationships that have been of value throughout my career and will continue to be critical in opening new markets, funding new ventures and driving the development of revolutionary new technologies.

"I bring to this position all the key management and leadership qualifications you require—strategic planning and business direction, technology development, multi-site operating management, P&L management, marketing, sales, capital raising, public relations, venture partner relations, team building and organizational development. These have been the backbone of my success to date and will continue to move my career forward as I continue to advance.

"One last point that I would like to leave you with is something that we have already discussed—my people skills. I can tell just from the short amount of time I have spent with you that you are also quite committed to your employees and appreciate their value and contributions. That is precisely the type of environment I am seeking ... a company where people are the foundation, technology is the market catalyst and positive results are the norm. This is certainly the perception I have gotten of TTT during this interview session."

What are your compensation requirements?

This is perhaps the most difficult of all questions to answer and requires more than just a paragraph or single page discussion of the topic. How do you negotiate an equitable compensation package, preferably larger than that which you are currently earning or earned in your most recent position without pricing yourself out of the running? How can you favorably negotiate incentives, stock options and an equity interest? What about signing bonuses and benefits?

Compensation negotiations can be the most challenging and daunting task of any interview. For a comprehensive discussion of this topic, refer to Chapter 6, *"Negotiating Winning Compensation Plans."*

THE FORBIDDEN FRUIT
Illegal Questions

In 1964, Title VII of the Civil Rights Acts was passed, making discrimination on the basis of race, sex, religion or national origin illegal in personnel hiring, promotion and decision making. Most interviewers are aware of these restrictions and will not ask illegal questions. If they do, generally it is because of their ignorance of the law.

Typical illegal questions include:

1. How old are you?

2. How many years until you retire?

3. Where were you born?

4. Where were your parents born?

5. What is your ancestry or lineage?

6. What is your race?

7. What is your native language?

8. Do you hold citizenship in any other country?

9. Are you married, divorced, separated or single?

10. Are you living with anyone?

11. Do you have children? Are they in day care?

12. How much do you weigh? How tall are you?

13. What color are your eyes? Your hair?

14. Have you ever legally changed your name?

15. What is your maiden name?

16. What is your political affiliation?

17. What is your religious affiliation?

18. What holidays do you celebrate?

19. Do you belong to any social or political groups?

20. What is your medical history?

21. Do you have any disabilities? What are they?

22. How does your disability affect your performance?

23. Have you ever filed a worker's compensation claim?

24. Have you ever been arrested?

25. Do you have a history of substance abuse?

26. Do you have a history of alcohol abuse?

27. What medications do you currently take?

28. What does your spouse think about your career?

29. Where does your spouse work?

30. Are you the primary wage earner for your family?

31. What are the names of your closest relatives?

32. Was your military discharge honorable?

33. What is your credit history?

34. Have you ever declared bankruptcy?

35. Have your wages ever been garnished?

If your interviewer asks these questions, you have two alternatives. You can bring to the interviewer's attention that the question is illegal and refuse to answer it. However, at that point, you will most likely alienate the interviewer and close the door on the potential opportunity. If you are really interested in the position, you may chose to answer the question, despite its illegality. Think carefully about your response so as not to provide any information that would exclude you from consideration. Then, make a mental note that once you have accepted the position, you will attempt to positively influence the hiring practices of the organization to meet all regulatory and legal requirements.

On rare occasions, an interviewer may ask these questions only to see your response and how well you manage a stressful situation. Although considered unethical as well as illegal, you should remain cool and even-tempered. You might inquire as to what relevance that question has to the position under discussion or use the opportunity to provide personal information that you believe is in your best interest. For example, if your interviewer inquires about your age, you may choose to give a straightforward answer. "I know that you are not allowed by law to ask that question, but I would be pleased to answer. I am 53 years old, in excellent condition, an avid golfer and tennis enthusiast, and just passed my last physical exam with flying colors."

With that answer, you have informed your interviewer that you are aware of the illegality of the question, but are quite interested in the position and willing to provide whatever type of information may be required. The interviewer should *"take the hint"* and steer clear of any further questions of that nature. Take the time, in advance, to think carefully about these illegal questions and what your responses will be if they are brought up in an interview.

QUESTIONS YOU SHOULD ASK

As we have discussed earlier, interviewing is a two-way street. Not only will the interviewer have a prepared list of questions for you, you should also have given serious consideration to what information you want from the company. This is a time for you to gather information so that you can make an informed decision.

Review the following questions and determine which are appropriate for each particular interview.

- What are the duties and responsibilities of this position?
- To whom will I report?
- Where does this position fit into the organization?
- What are the supervisory, managerial and leadership responsibilities of the position?
- Why is the incumbent leaving this position?
- What type of qualities would your ideal candidate bring to the position and to your organization?
- What type of experience and qualifications are you seeking in a candidate?
- What problems might I expect to encounter in relation to job function and personnel?
- May I speak with present and past employees to get their feedback?

- How long have you been with the company?
- How long has the President/CEO been with the company? What about other members of the executive team?
- What is the greatest challenge that the company faces today?
- What are the company's 1-, 5- and 10-year plans?
- Why is this position so critical to the company's immediate and long-term success?
- Tell me about advancement and promotional opportunities.
- What is the salary, bonus and compensation for this position?

6
Negotiating Winning Compensation Plans

Negotiating compensation can be the single most difficult component of your executive job search campaign. How can you negotiate a higher salary than that which you are currently earning without pushing yourself out of the running? How can you determine your worth to a specific organization? Have you ever considered a lower salary in exchange for an equity interest? What is the cumulative value of the benefits the company has to offer? Is the company willing to pay for performance and results?

There are so many considerations in negotiating an equitable compensation package and each must be addressed individually. It is imperative that you remember that the compensation package you negotiate today will impact your future earnings for years and years to come. A good rule of thumb if you are currently employed is that you can expect a salary averaging 10% to 15% over your current earnings.

Salary discussions can be extremely awkward. Your goal is to negotiate the best compensation possible. Your interviewer's goal is to control hiring and compensation costs. Immediately, there is disparity between your objectives which can lead to disparity in your negotiations. It is vital that you remember that most positions do not have a predetermined salary level and that most employers are flexible and willing to negotiate a fair compensation package to attract the right talent to their organization. Although their objective may be to control costs, their primary objective is a successful executive hire.

Executive job search candidates must remember that compensation is generally NOT a discussion addressed in the first interview. The objective of the first interview is to determine whether or not you have the qualifications for the position. It is a time that you and the company *"get to know each other,"* allowing the interviewer to assess whether or not you have the professional qualifications, personal characteristics, attitude and behavior they are seeking in a qualified candidate. Compensation discussions are usually, although not always, reserved for further in the interview process—perhaps interview #2, #3 or even #4.

It is very difficult to discuss compensation prior to a full understanding of the responsibilities and accountabilities of the position for which you are interviewing. If your interviewer does bring up compensation during interview #1, you might consider asking to delay that conversation until such time as you have learned more about the position and the company. About 50% of the time, the interviewer will agree; the other 50%, he/she will push you for an answer.

Prior to a salary discussion, you should have done your homework. What do other companies in the same industry or market pay executives in this type of position? What do national salary surveys indicate? What are other executives in the company being compensated? The latter may be more difficult to determine if the company is not publicly-held and compensation is privileged information. The more information you can amass, the better equipped you will be to negotiate a favorable compensation package.

Compensation discussions often begin with the interviewer asking you, "What are your salary requirements?" One of the best strategies to deploy at this point is to respond with, "What was the salary range you had in mind?" This pushes the onus back onto the interviewer to at least give you some indication of what they expect to pay an executive in this position. The interviewer may respond with, "The range we are willing to consider is $95,000 to $125,000." Obviously, your answer is always, "The high end of the range is certainly in line with my expectations." The only time that this answer would not be appropriate would be if the compensation was significantly lower than what you are currently making, had recently made or were anticipating for the position.

If you know that you will be replacing someone currently in the position (they are retiring, have accepted a new opportunity, have been promoted or have been dismissed), you might ask, "What is the incumbent currently being compensated?" Again, the onus is back on the interviewer to give you some idea of what the salary may be.

If, however, your interviewer is not able to or not willing to share the above information with you, you must then respond with specific information regarding your requirements. The best strategy at this point is to mention your current or most recent compensation as a starting point. You might offer, "In my current position as Vice President of Technology, my base salary is $150,000 with an annual bonus ranging from $25,000 to $45,000. In addition, I have stock options, bringing my total compensation to just over $225,000 annually."

It is also recommended that you prepare a written statement of your current, or most recent, compensation package. Instead of simply stating that your current compensation package is $225,000, prepare a typewritten document that breaks down each component of your current package. You might include last year's versus this year's or this year's versus next year's compensation. This provides your interviewer with specific information that he/she can review and use as a baseline for the offer that they will be making to you.

When the salary topic is finally raised, and you have a more detailed understanding of the position, you will be better equipped to respond. Begin your answer with a brief summary of the position as you understand it:

"As I understand, the position of CIO will report directly to the President and be accountable for the strategic and tactical leadership of the entire information technology function. I will be responsible for a $32 million annual operating budget, a team of more than 200 individuals and a direct management reporting staff of 10." A statement of this type clearly defines the level of position, financial accountability, supervisory responsibility and value of the position to the company. It is a great point for leveraging favorable and financially rewarding compensation discussions.

NEGOTIATING & ACCEPTING THE OFFER

For executive job seekers, serious compensation discussions are generally delayed well into the interview process, close to the time or at the time the company is making you an offer. Unlike in your earlier positions, where salary was principally the only point of negotiation, executives must negotiate an entire compensation package that may include a combination of base salary, benefits, stock options, equity interest, signing bonus, performance bonus and pension/retirement plan. Each point must be carefully evaluated and individually addressed.

When the time to discuss compensation finally does arrive, your best strategy is to listen carefully to what the interviewer is offering. Offers may be presented verbally, but are generally presented in writing. At this point, you have four basic options in response to the company's financial offer:

1. Accept it as it is presented and the negotiations are finalized.

2. Negotiate for additional compensation in the form of increased base salary, an equity interest, stock options, incentives or an expanded benefits program.

3. Ask for time to think about the offer.

4. Turn the offer down, thank the interviewer for his/her time and leave.

Options #1 and #4 are not recommended. With #1, you may appear too anxious and, in turn, too desperate. With #4, you have forever put yourself out of the running for the position.

Options #2 and #3 are your best strategy. With #2, you are demonstrating that you are an educated job seeker fully aware of your worth. Most companies expect that you will negotiate; it's part of the *"executive job search game."* Clearly state the specific areas that you would like the company to reconsider (e.g., base salary, signing bonus) and why you are worth more than they are offering. You can expect to negotiate key points back and forth until a mutually-agreed upon package is finalized. Remember, at this point, you are somewhat in control. The company wants you! Use that to your advantage without exploiting it. Be fair in your compensation requests, not outrageous. How you manage these negotiations will establish the precedent for how you will manage future negotiations with and on behalf of the company. This is the time to demonstrate your savvy, poise, professionalism and determination. This is the time to show the company your ability to drive forward successful negotiations where both parties are satisfied and both parties are winners.

Option #3 is also an accepted practice. Once you have received an offer, you can ask your interviewer for a few days to consider it. Forty-eight hours is a normal time by which the company will most likely expect a response. Take this time to consider the compensation that has been offered, the potential for increased earnings, any other offers you have received or anticipate receiving, and all of the other particulars of the position. Will you be proud to be associated with the company? Were you impressed with the caliber of the other executives? Is the company's financial position solid? What is the company's reputation in the market? Will you be happy?

After you have considered all of the above, and any other relevant issues, contact the company and either accept the employment offer or initiate negotiations as in item #2 above. Just because you have asked for time to consider the offer does not mean that you must accept it exactly as it is presented. Remember, the higher the level of position, the more intricate the compensation package, and the more likely that negotiations will result.

SALARY, BENEFITS & YOUR COMPENSATION PLAN

As with any other business negotiation, your objective is to get the most you possibly can. Be sure that everything you agree on is clearly documented in your employment contract (see next section). You want to maximize your base salary, benefits package, bonus opportunity and participation in company stock-related and deferred compensation programs. It is at this point where the information you have obtained relative to the compensation of the company's existing executive team will be of most value to you. And, despite all the conversation about your value to the organization and what a difference you will make, nothing demonstrates that more than when the pen hits the paper.

Base Salary

Base salary is almost always the #1 consideration when negotiating an equitable compensation package. If you are currently employed, you should expect a 10% to 15% increase over your existing base salary. This is also true if you have only recently left your last position. However, if you have been in the job search market for an extended period of time, this may not be the case. You will have to give serious consideration to the offer being made and not simply accept it out of desperation. Only you know your personal financial situation and only you can make an appropriate decision.

In your employment contract, be sure that you are guaranteed *"a base salary of at least X with annual performance reviews."* In certain circumstances, base salary increases will be formally addressed in the interview, in the offer and in your employment contract.

Employee Benefits

Traditional employee benefits are a vital component of every compensation plan. These will almost always include health, dental, disability and life insurance, and a pension or retirement plan. Also be sure to review the company's personal leave policy. These standard benefits are generally offered to ALL of the company's employees (albeit various options).

More recently, in an effort to attract qualified personnel and in response to underlying political currents, many companies have expanded their traditional benefit packages to include vision care, tax-free health care spending accounts, child day care, elder day care, and spousal life and disability insurance programs. Most of these are optional and will have an associated cost to you. Carefully review each offering to determine its relevance to your particular life situation.

Executive Benefits

After base salary, this is where you can MAKE THE MONEY! At the executive level, you can anticipate a combination of the following:

Bonus

Executive bonuses, just like those offered to other employees, should be based on your performance or the specific function or business unit for which you are accountable. Do not negotiate a bonus dependent upon the performance of an organization over which you have no control.

If you are currently in an employment situation where you are virtually guaranteed a bonus, make sure that you brought this to the attention of the hiring company during your initial compensation discussions. It is recommended that you negotiate a first-year guarantee to ensure that you will receive an equivalent performance bonus. If possible, negotiate a bonus of 10% to 30% over that which you would receive in your current position—another incentive to accept the new opportunity.

Signing Bonus

An attractive executive benefit is the signing bonus or one-time bonus. This can be used to cover your relocation costs (if appropriate) or as an incentive to lure you from your current position. Signing bonuses can vary widely in dollar value, from just a few thousand to tens of thousands of dollars depending upon the situation and your value to that company.

Stock Option Plans

These plans are widely used as employee incentives and/or part of an employee compensation package, and are usually reserved for the executives of a corporation. The executive is given an option to purchase the corporation's shares at a certain price (at or below the market price at the time the option is granted) for a specified period of time.

Stock option plans can vary widely from one organization to another, and often companies will have several plans operating simultaneously. They may include incentive stock options, nonqualified stock options, stock grants, stock appreciation rights, phantom stock options, stock purchase plans and other alternatives.

Profit Sharing Plans

These plans are agreements that allow employees, generally executives, to share in a company's profits. Annual contributions are made by the company, when it has profits, to a profit sharing account for each executive, either in cash or through a deferred contribution plan.

Deferred Compensation Plans

These types of plans are a means of supplementing an executive's retirement benefits by deferring a portion of his/her current earnings. Deferring income like this encourages employee loyalty and longevity. For these types of plans to qualify as a tax advantage, the IRS requires a written agreement between an executive and his employer stating the specified period of time for income deferral. This type of plan is irrevocable and must be made prior to the start of your employment.

Deferred Contribution Plans

These plans are negotiated arrangements in which an unused deduction (credit carryover) to a profit sharing plan can be added to a future contribution on a tax deductible basis. Deferred contributions can be taken as stock shares, bonds or a cash equivalent. These plans are applicable only when an employer's contribution to the profit sharing plan is less than the annual 15% of an employee's total compensation as allowed by the Federal Tax Code.

Equity Participation

If you are offered a position as one of the top executives of a corporation, you may also be offered equity participation, an actual ownership interest in the company. If you believe that the company has significant financial potential, this can be an extremely rewarding benefit generally reserved exclusively for the *"top team."* Often this type of benefit is offered in what many may consider a high risk situation. Just remember, high risk often translates into high reward. If the risk is such that you are willing to accept the position, then you should most likely be interested in equity participation. Be advised, however, that equity is often offered in exchange for dollars from your pocket. Only you can determine your level of comfort with this option.

Golden Parachute

These are a relatively new phenomena that have arisen as a result of the massive prevalence of corporate mergers, acquisitions and takeovers. In theory, these plans are designed to *"take care of you"* if you are let go or demoted as a result of a corporate transition.

Golden parachutes can be golden! They will most likely include:

- one to five years of your highest base plus bonus annual compensation (your choice of lump sum or payment over time)

- immediate vesting of and access to stock (you can either retain it as an investment or sell it back to the company at the *"hopefully"* inflated takeover price)

- immediate vesting of pension benefits

- immediate exercise of all options

- immediate payment of all performance bonuses and incentives

- continuation of company-paid medical and life insurance for the same duration as your compensation, or until such time as you accept a new position.

Golden Handcuffs

Be forewarned. There are also compensation programs that make it quite costly for you to leave the company. Certain options and incentive schemes require that you stay with the company for an extended period of time to get the benefit of what you are *"earning"* now. These types of programs are devised specifically to protect the employer—not the executive employee.

TAKE NOTE! If you are not well versed in stock options plans, deferred compensation plans, deferred contributions plans, pension plans, profit sharing plans and other executive benefit programs, contact an attorney, accountant or financial advisor who can help you evaluate your specific options. These are critical decisions that impact your immediate and long-term earnings, and should be carefully researched to make an educated decision.

In reference to the above discussion, consider that smaller companies, new ventures and emerging enterprises may not be in a position to offer such a plethora of benefit programs. In this instance, you may be offered a higher base salary to compensate for the lack of benefits or may be offered an attractive equity participation program when your efforts will have a direct impact upon the company's performance. This can be a potentially risky situation. Only you can determine your own *"risk-to-reward"* quotient that you can comfortably live with.

EXECUTIVE EMPLOYMENT CONTRACTS

We would all like to think that a verbal agreement and handshake are just as good as a written contract. They're not. To protect yourself and your family, you will want to get all of the terms of your employment and compensation in writing. Employment contracts, once a rarity, are increasingly becoming the norm, particularly for the executive job seeker.

Are employment contracts the same as offer letters? No, but they are quite similar. Both spell out the terms and conditions of your employment, your compensation package and other relevant information. However, the more senior the position, the more complex the terms of the agreement and the more likely that not only will you receive an offer letter, but also an employment contract.

If you are provided only an offer letter, do not be alarmed. If problems, issues or litigation arise between you and the employer, the offer letter will be invaluable in substantiating your claims (assuming your claims are valid based upon the specifics of your employment as stated in the offer letter). Be advised that you will almost always receive a formal offer letter. It is accepted business practice today.

> **WARNING ! ! !**
> Do not resign your current position until you have received, in writing, an offer from a new employer.

Assuming that you are being offered a very senior level opportunity, you can also expect to receive an employment contract which should include:

- Length of the Contract
- Position Title & Reporting Accountability
- Your Specific Duties & Responsibilities
- Termination Issues
- Compensation Package

The first issue, and one of the most significant, to be negotiated is the length of the employment contract. Your goal will most likely be a multi-year contract, guaranteeing employment for three years, five years, perhaps even longer. However, the agenda of the company will most likely be for a shorter period of time—generally one year. The employer wants to retain the freedom and flexibility to change the executive team as may be necessary due to market and economic conditions, competitive influences, financial obligations and liabilities, and other major factors impacting the company's performance and stability. In this situation, compromise is the key to agreement. You may have to decrease your expectations while the company increases their commitment.

If an employer wants to ensure your long-term tenure with the company, he/she may include an automatic renewal clause which can extend the contract indefinitely. It may be worded much like *"This contract shall be extended for an additional three years unless either party notifies the other, in writing, at least six months prior to the termination of this agreement."*

Your employment contract should not only include your job title and whom you will be reporting to, but also a detailed listing of all of your job responsibilities (much like a position description). Where will you be working? Will you be elected to the Board of Directors? Will you serve on the Management Committee? What are your bottom-line financial accountabilities? What functions, departments or organizations will report to you? Which employees will report to you? Be wary of phrases such as *"duties as may be assigned"* which are vague and open to vastly different interpretations.

Once in writing, this part of the document serves to clearly state what you are accountable for and to whom. If there is ever any question, both you and the employer can refer to this document to clarify any issues.

The fourth component of your employment contract is related to termination. Again, you and the employer will approach this negotiation with vastly differing agendas. Your objective is to agree to termination only for illegal acts or blatant negligence. On the other side of the table, the employer wants the flexibility to be able to terminate your employment for virtually any reason once the length of the contract has been fulfilled. In this situation, the employer will usually win. Generally, the only safeguard you will be able to negotiate is length of contract.

Your compensation package is the other most vital component of your employment contract. As discussed previously, it is imperative that every single component of your compensation be clearly documented in your contract. This may include base salary, performance and signing bonuses, stock options, pension plans, golden parachute plans and other executive incentives.

Two other vital considerations in negotiating your employment contract are related to non-competitive and confidentiality issues. The employer wants to ensure that you will not be easily attracted to another company much like theirs (non-compete) and wants to protect their trade secrets, products, market intelligence and other proprietary information (confidentiality).

When negotiating these elements of your employment contract, your objective is to make sure that they are fair to you. Obviously, the company is biased and will attempt to make these extremely restrictive and to their benefit. Not only may your non-compete agreement cover the length of your employment contract, it may extend for years beyond. Note that this can be a great bargaining tool for you. If you're so much in demand, the company will, of course, want to pay you dearly.

To protect yourself in a non-compete agreement, the first step is to try to eliminate it all together. If that is not possible, it is advised that you negotiate the following:

- The clause is void if you are fired or your contract is not renewed.

- The clause prevents full-time work, not part-time consulting.

- The clause includes only companies that are in direct competition.

Be particularly careful in relation to the confidentiality clause. If the agreement is so pervasive and prevents you from discussing virtually anything about the company, it will be very easy to terminate you for the slightest mention of any information. Attempt to negotiate a contract that simply states *"intentional disclosures that could be harmful to the company."*

Both non-compete and confidentiality agreements are very difficult to legally enforce unless the company can demonstrate financial damage through loss of market share, loss of customers, loss of revenues or loss of profits. However, there is an ethical issue here that cannot be overlooked. When you sign an employment contract in good faith, you are pledging your honesty and your loyalty to the company. It is *"understood"* that you should not take their trade secrets to a competitive organization, divulge privileged information or share data regarding a pending patent. If you do, you are placing yourself in a potentially liable situation and may have to pay the consequences.

It is highly recommended that you consult legal counsel prior to signing an employment contract. The minimal cost of attorney's fees is well worth the expense. Not only are you protecting yourself, you are ensuring that the contract does state exactly what you understand has been negotiated. A wise job seeker uses all the appropriate resources. In this instance, an attorney is vital.

SUMMARY

Just as you feel confident in your professional competencies, you must also learn to be a confident negotiator. Know your financial worth and clearly present that worth to your interviewer. There is no one that will advocate on your behalf; only you. Do not settle for less than you are worth, hoping that in a short while the company will come to understand and appreciate your value, and be willing to offer a more attractive compensation package at that time. What you negotiate today will be the foundation for your compensation with the company for years and years to come. It will also be the precedent for your future earnings.

Keep the following strategies, concepts, tips and techniques in the forefront when the infamous salary negotiations arise.

If at all possible, allow the interviewer to raise the topic of compensation; not you.

Attempt to delay salary discussions until you are well into the interview process. If pushed, you can simply respond with the fact that your salary requirements are open, negotiable or flexible.

An easy way for interviewers to screen out potential candidates is by raising the salary issue early in your discussions. This can be an extremely efficient strategy to eliminate potential candidates who are *"overpriced."*

You must be able to clearly state why you are worth a specific salary or compensation package. This is best accomplished with specific examples of your past performance, level of responsibility and notable achievements (as they directly relate to the company with which you are interviewing).

If, in your original discussions with the company, you stated that your current compensation package was $145,000 per year, stand by that number throughout all of your negotiations. If, after four interviews and an offer, you comment that although your base was $145,000, you also received an annual bonus of approximately $35,000, negotiations will most likely come to an abrupt halt. Why? It is not necessarily because of the additional $35,000, but rather the fact that you misled the company in your initial discussions. More than likely, the offer will be rescinded.

If an offer is made by one company and you are currently in the final interview stages with another company, contact the latter to let them know that you have received an offer. Give them the opportunity to make a counter-offer if they are able to reach a decision. This can only be to your professional and financial advantage.

Always remember that the ultimate purpose of your interview is to demonstrate your worth to a prospective employer. Do not attempt to translate your worth into dollars until such time as you have been successful in communicating your value to that organization.

7
Winning
Follow-Up Strategies

Once an interview has concluded, there are several courses of action that you must immediately follow to keep your name at the top of the list of qualified candidates and ensure that you are invited back for another interview and, eventually, are extended an offer. Devote the effort necessary to:

- produce powerful thank you letters.
- follow-up on the telephone.
- leverage your contact network.

POWER THANK YOU LETTERS

There are two types of thank you letters—traditional and power. The former is what you probably think of when someone mentions a thank you letter. It's just a quick note to acknowledge the time an individual spent interviewing you and telling them you look forward to meeting with them (or someone higher up in the organization) again.

Power thank you letters serve the same purpose while providing you with the opportunity to again sell your product—YOU. They are more aggressive and include more information to sell you into the position. Power letters have three distinct purposes:

1. **To bring attention to the specific skills, qualifications, experiences and achievements you bring to the table that are directly related to the requirements of the position and the needs of the company.** Think of your power thank you letter as a second stage marketing tool, highlighting the features and benefits of the product most attractive to that specific audience.

2. **To overcome objections.** The power thank you letter is the ideal platform to discuss the company's concerns relative to your qualifications, background, market knowledge, product knowledge, industry experience and related topics. Again, the letter is a tool that, when used wisely, can favorably present information that may previously have been considered a liability.

3. **To ask for either the next interview or the offer.** This will depend upon what stage of the interview process you are in. Be forthright about your interest in the company and the position.

SAMPLE THANK YOU LETTERS

On the following pages, you'll find sample thank you letters that clearly follow the purposes outlined above. Please feel free to use these letters as guidelines for your own thank you letters, to leave a lasting impression with your potential employer.

JOSHUA E. JONES
189 Meredith Way
Meridian, California 94444

Phone: (619) 999-3333   Email: jej@aol.com

May 2, 1998

Mr. Robert Lawrence
President
Newtown Equity, Inc.
190 Wabash Avenue
Chicago, IL 66666

Dear Bob:

Since our meeting last Monday, I have given careful thought to our conversation and the tremendous market opportunities that are opening for Newtown. I am fully confident that I will succeed in building a strong and successful business development team. Let me take just a moment to address a few key points.

First and foremost, I am a "dealmaker" and marketer, able to capture market opportunities and deliver strong revenue and asset performance. I tackle each new project with a two-pronged focus: (1) negotiate the best possible transaction that is truly a "win-win" for each partner; and (2) create strategic and tactical marketing programs that achieve a strong and sustainable competitive position.

We have spoken at length about my achievements in new business development, new ventures, asset management and asset growth. We have discussed my success in structuring and negotiating complex financial transactions, improving cash flow and strengthening partner relationships. Enough talk; now it's time for action.

You're right. I have never worked in the Chicago market. However, I have demonstrated my ability to build presence in other markets nationwide (e.g., Minneapolis, St. Louis, Phoenix, Charlotte). Further, I have an extensive network of contacts across the country, many of whom are well connected in Chicago and are more than willing to introduce me around town.

I have always been fortunate. Networking is a natural process for me. I am able to quickly ascertain who it is that I must establish a relationship with, identify the appropriate channels to do so, and quickly begin the process. In turn, despite often unfamiliar territories and personalities, I have quickly established myself in key markets. I am not daunted by challenge, but rather motivated to succeed and beat the odds.

I hope that you and I have the opportunity to continue our discussions. Thank you again for your time and your support.

Sincerely,

Joshua E. Jones

JERRY NELSON
899 Portage Road
Portland, Maine 09938
(372) 992-3827

September 11, 1998

Lou Montgomery
President
RSC Corporation
193 RSC Drive
Rochester, NY 19388

Dear Lou:

Last month's unveiling of RSC's new corporate structure clearly indicates that the "dust is beginning to settle" and it's time to get back to business. Not only do I appreciate your tremendous commitment of time and energy to get this project moving forward, but also the enormous effort involved in building a new management team to lead RSC through its next stage of growth. Congratulations! It's been lots of work from which I hope you feel both personal and professional satisfaction.

When we last spoke, you indicated there would be an opportunity for me with RSC and I'm still anticipating that position. In the interim, I have continued to move my search forward and am at various interviewing stages with several corporations. Although a few of these opportunities are exciting, none offer the potential that is evident with RSC. As such, I need your help in clarifying the time frame for my entry into RSC.

Let's not reiterate my achievements. You already know. What I will share with you is what I have learned throughout my career … that success lies in one's ability to merge the strategic with the tactical, to understand the markets, to know the competition and to build a strong and performance-driven management team. No one function is solely accountable for results. It is the integration of everything and the combined strength of the leadership team.

That is what I bring to RSC – the ability to "get my hands around" the entire picture, leverage opportunities, build markets and advance technologies. With the support of my staff and business team, I guarantee to deliver results.

I thrive in challenging, high-energy and high-performance organizations, much like the "new" RSC. Further, I remain highly committed to the challenges and opportunities that await me with the organization and anxiously look forward to your call. Let me assure you that the strength of my leadership experience and track record of performance will be a solid asset for RSC's new management team.

Sincerely,

Jerry Nelson

Jerry Nelson

ALEXIS E. McCALL

9 North Green Street
Market Town, PA 19877
(215) 383-2522

December 18, 1998

George P. Smith
President & CEO
AAA Technologies
777 87th Boulevard
Plano, TX 77877

Dear Mr. Smith:

First of all, thank you. I thoroughly enjoyed the time I spent with you and your management team during my recent visit to AAA. The commitment that each of you has to your employees and, in turn, their commitment to the company is remarkably unusual and admirable in this age of constant corporate change and reorganization.

Yes, I want to be a part of the AAA management team – in whatever capacity you feel most appropriate and of most value. As a senior HR professional, my efforts have focused largely on the resources and value of the workforce, and what I can do to optimize productivity, build camaraderie, recognize excellence and contribute to bottom-line profitability.

Perhaps the most critical lesson I have learned over the years is to "not fix that which is not broken." In this regard, I am referring to the corporate culture you have created and which I believe has been the foundation for much of AAA's success. Therefore, it is not my intention to change that which already exists; rather, my goal is to nurture that culture and your employees to even greater heights of performance.

Although we have discussed the following HR issues to some degree, there are several key points I would like to address:

- "**2000 Employees by Year 2000**" is an aggressive but realistic goal to which I bring significant value. As the first HR executive with Grossman Financial, I created the entire recruitment and selection process, bringing more than 100 employees into the company. With Excel, I spearheaded recruitment for operations in both the US and Europe. For Baxter, I launched an initiative to recruit 450 professionals to our engineering organization. In sum, my recruitment efforts have focused on managerial, technical, professional and administrative talent.

- **Acquisition integration** is another area in which I have solid experience to support AAA's aggressive M&A program. Knowing the success of your existing organizational culture, it is imperative that the individuals retained are completely assimilated into the existing culture, becoming viable and productive contributors within a relatively short period of time. I have met this type of challenge before and will continue to do so for AAA.

George P. Smith
December 18, 1998
Page Two

- **International business affairs and expansion** has been one of my key management responsibilities. Specifically, I directed international recruitment, staffing and generalist HR affairs for more than 1000 expatriate and foreign national employees of the LSY Company. I am sensitive and responsive to cultural differences and successful in optimizing those differences to strengthen overall performance. As AAA continues to expand, this will become an increasingly important management function in driving profitable international growth.

The goals that AAA has outlined for the immediate and long-term growth of the corporation require strong HR leadership today. The optimum path is to bring a professional into the organization, assimilate them into the existing culture, and allow them to initiate the plans and actions to support profitable growth and expansion. I would like to be that individual, responsible for building the leadership and technical talent that will successfully lead AAA into the future.

On a more personal note, the value I bring to AAA is more than just my HR and organizational leadership experience. Just as significant has been my career path which has taken me from the "ground floor" through the ranks to my most senior management position. As a result of these vastly differing experiences, I am able to build camaraderie and trust throughout all levels of an organization. The saying, "I have been there and done that" is true and provides the workforce with a sense of security in my decision making and leadership capabilities.

I hope that this information is of interest to you and has further demonstrated my value to AAA. I look forward to continuing our discussion and thank you again for your time and consideration.

Sincerely,

Alexis E. McCall

Alexis E. McCall

ANDREW W. WILLIAMS
73838 Drake Drive
Danbury, Florida 32292
(954) 393-3902

July 11, 1998

Richard Bartlett
Director
Executive Recruitment, Inc.
191 Elm Road
Edna, Florida 32987

Dear Dick:

Thanks for the conversation and the preliminary interview. I'm quite interested in the executive sales and marketing position with the Lee Corporation and
would like to aggressively pursue the opportunity. I've been searching "quietly" for
a new position for several months and this is really the first assignment that has
sparked my interest. Now, I'd like to take a few minutes to highlight my success in
sales, marketing and customer management as it directly relates to the position
with Lee.

As one of only four executives with SY-4 Technology, not only was I responsible for selling and marketing the company, its products and its technologies, I was
also one of the key drivers in the customer service/support organization. In addition, I was the lead contact for many major customers and am personally credited
with closing over $200 million in sales with key corporate clients (e.g., AOL, Federal
Express, Siemens, Westinghouse).

My most significant contribution has been the recapture and resurrection of
the General Electric account, now SY-4's largest and most profitable customer. To
understand the impact of this achievement, we have to go back four years when GE
was in the process of telling SY-4 it was going to change vendors (after a six-year
relationship). GE was in California to present the "loss story" to our executives and
I was asked to step in.

The situation was difficult. The CEO had attempted an unsuccessful turnaround, yet the company was committed to keeping the account. They gave me a
challenge and I delivered. I made an immediate (that afternoon) proposal to GE
based on a new architecture under development which met all of their critical
objectives. They traveled to another one of our locations, they believed in what I
promised and they bought. GE now generates over $80 million in revenues each
year and are expected to exceed $100 million next year.

I can relate similar success stories with other accounts – Federal Express,
Marriott, Square D. The lead role I played with each of these, and others, has been
one of the major contributors to SY-4's success.

Richard Bartlett
July 11, 1998
Page Two

Let me also bring to your attention that I have substantial experience in product management and product marketing. As VP of the Systems Division, I was directly responsible for product strategy, development and management for much of the company's first five years (the period of highest growth and profitability).

Over the past two years my focus has been the aggressive turnaround, market repositioning and growth of our new UNIX Division. I transitioned our market focus to the emerging telecommunications industry and established marketing teams to capture key players and channel partners. Results have been strong with record sales in 1996.

Further demonstrating my performance in selling, marketing negotiating and closing, has been my leadership of several key mergers and acquisitions. Most notably, I was asked to finalize the sale of assets and intellectual property that was being negotiated by the new CEO. Negotiations had stalled and I was brought in. Under my leadership, we closed the deal and had a check in 72 hours, just in time to post positive financial results for year-end.

In closing, it is appropriate to point out that one of the keys of good selling is good listening. If you do not understand your clients' needs and expectations, the relationship will never grow and the partnership will never solidify. This is perhaps the greatest value I bring to any organization; my ability to "hear" what a customer is saying and respond with the "right" products, services and support.

I'm excited about this opportunity and look forward to continuing our discussions. I await your immediate response.

Sincerely,

Andrew W. Williams

Andrew W. Williams

WINNING TELEPHONE FOLLOW-UP STRATEGIES

If, after a specified period of time, you have not heard back from the company, it is recommended that you follow-up with a telephone call. When you call will depend upon when the interviewer said they would be in back in touch with you. If you were told you would be contacted within a month and four weeks have passed, pick up the phone and call. If no specific period of time was offered, wait two to three weeks and then call.

Use your time wisely on the telephone. Reiterate your interest in the position and the company, and briefly highlight one or two items about your experience that you feel are of most value to that organization. Tell them you want the position. Ask how they are proceeding in the interview process, if they have made any decisions and when you can expect to hear from them. Tell them you would welcome the chance to meet with the executive team again and have the opportunity to further expand upon your skills and experiences. Consider this a marketing follow-up call. Be professional, yet assertive in moving the process forward.

Often it is quite difficult to get the person you wish to speak with on the telephone. It may be that individual is extremely busy and filling the position is not #1 on his/her list of priorities. It may be that they are still actively recruiting and interviewing, and are not ready to offer anyone a second interview yet. Or, it may be that person is attempting to avoid you, knowing that for whatever reason, you are no longer being considered for the position.

If you find that you are having difficulty getting someone on the phone, feel free to leave one or two messages; no more. If you do not hear back from them, chances are likely that you are no longer in the running, that the company has decided not to hire, or any one of a number of other reasons. Let it go. Do not continue to call over and over. It will not do any good. If the company is interested in you, they will follow-up.

Do not be surprised, however, if six weeks later, after no contact, you get a phone call to come in for another interview. Often the hiring process takes much longer than anyone would anticipate either because of time constraints, the number of qualified candidates, or other more critical projects and responsibilities. In the meantime, make sure that you have been aggressively continuing your job search efforts with more networking, more ad responses, an expanded direct mailing effort or new Internet postings. Always keep your search moving forward until you are sitting at your new desk in your new office. A comment from an interviewer stating that your qualifications look great and that you are indeed a top candidate really means nothing until such time that you have an offer letter in your hand. Never slow your search down despite what anyone may say.

LEVERAGE YOUR CONTACT NETWORK

If you were networked into or recommended for an interview, get in touch with your contact immediately after the interview. Tell him/her how the interview progressed, interesting facts you learned about the company or the individual you interviewed with, and how you think things went overall. Be enthusiastic and express your interest in the position. Then ask your contact if he/she would be willing to make a follow-up phone call to see what the company's impressions were. Did they like you? What did they identify as your potential shortcomings or weaknesses? Are they considering you? Are they going to offer you a second interview? Where did you stack up against the competition?

This type of market intelligence can be invaluable in guiding your future communications and interviews with that company. Hopefully, your contact will get back to you quickly with specific information. Take his/her positive comments and work to even further leverage and favorably exploit them with the company. When you write your power thank you letter, make sure to mention the top one or two, and how your experience in those areas will translate into success for the company. Take the negative comments, think hard about your responses and work to overcome those objections. Explain why they are not liabilities, but rather can be of value to the organization or can be transitioned into more favorable attributes.

Perhaps most importantly, ask your contact to *"put in a good word"* on your behalf. It can only work to your advantage.

If your contact is not willing to phone the company, ask if he/she would be willing to write a quick note. You'll still benefit from the *"good word,"* albeit a bit more passively. In this situation, you will not be able to wait until your contact gets back to you with information and ideas to work into your power thank you letter. You'll have to move forward and hope that your insights are in line with the company's needs, expectations and impression of you.

8

Tips from the Top

A s with any topic on job search—resumes, cover letters, direct mail, the Internet and more—there are many opinions about interviewing. Everyone involved in the job search arena has different ideas, strategies, tools and techniques for interview success. Each believes that his/her suggestions and recommendations are vital to your success in today's tremendously competitive executive job search market.

Following are "Tips From The Top"—proven success strategies for proactively managing the interview process and positioning yourself as the #1 candidate. Review the comments and recommendations of these human resource executives, outplacement executives, recruiters, resume writers, career coaches and others. Each of these individuals has earned a reputation for success in interviewing and job search, and was willing to share his/her insights with you.

Kent Black, an Executive Career Consultant in San Rafael, California, former Group Vice President with Drake Beam Morin and former Senior Vice President with J. Walter Thompson tells us,

"Creating rapport and identifying common background are critical to establishing a strong connection during senior level interviewing. Such a foundation combined with the ability to comfortably align one's principles to those of the corporation are the basic requirements for a mutually successful interview at the senior level.

"As in all interviewing, it is important to be well versed on the needs of the interviewer and the company as well as being prepared to extol your skills and abilities particularly as they relate to being the best candidate for the job. However, interviewees at the senior level frequently have comparable skills, experience and functional abilities. Therefore, it is the ability to create a connection to the personality of the interviewer and the culture of the company that will determine who is selected.

"It is well documented that good interpersonal skills are absolutely mandatory in the senior executive ranks and are often MORE important than any particular technical or functional set of skills. Extensive research done by the Center for Creative Learning and the Manchester Group found that 40% of senior executive new hires fail within 18 months principally because of the executives' lack of ability to effectively manage direct reports or relate well with peers. The inability to manage the boss and function in a politically savvy way came in second in the ranking of reasons why the relationships failed. Failure to meet objectives was a comparatively weak third in this ranking.

"**Common Ground**—If you have background, interests or history that the interviewer can easily relate to, it is amazing how quickly formalities and barriers melt, and an aura of openness in communications is established. For example, if you were born in the same area, or went to the same school, or share similar work experiences or interests in sports and hobbies, or have volunteered time to causes and charities that have similar purposes, a commonality is established that creates a more relaxed and friendly atmosphere. A positive rapport will pave the way for an effective interview experience. Be sure to cover these bases in your answer to the almost always asked question, 'Tell me about yourself.'

"**Compatible Chemistry**—Evaluate how you relate to the people you interview with and/or just meet in the interview process. Are these people with whom you would like to spend time, not only on the job but also socially? Recognize that not all will or have to pass the social criteria, but it is a good place to start an assessment. If there is no one you would like to socialize with, then you are probably in the wrong company.

"**Cultural Fit**—Are you in agreement with the company's values, mission statement, overall purpose and future direction? What can you find out or what do you know about their history in this very important area? Does this company 'walk the talk' or are these conviction-driven principles either non-existent or only for show? If your due diligence reveals a good 'fit' between the beliefs and values most important to you, then the likelihood of a successful connection with this company is increased.

"The issue of whether you 'can do' or have the 'will to do' the job, while obviously important, are often not as significant as how well you 'fit' the culture of the organization."

Dave Theobald, President of Netshare, Inc. (publisher of executive job lead reports) in Novato, California, and former executive recruiter shares the following:

"Remember, THE INTERVIEW IS NEVER OVER. A 'trick' I used when I was in the search business would be to conclude the interview and suggest we have lunch, a drink or whatever was appropriate. I could see the candidate relax and offer a sigh of relief. Then over lunch (or the drink), he would proceed to tell me things that gave me the right insight of who he really was including things he shouldn't have—he forgot that the interview was never over.

"It is also critical that you remember that if there isn't a chemistry, culture or philosophical fit, FORGET IT! Don't rationalize this and kid yourself into believing that you can either fix or live with whatever it is that isn't totally comfortable."

Jay Block, a Certified Job & Career Transition Coach and Certified Professional Resume Writer in West Palm Beach, Florida, and Past Executive Board Member of the Professional Association of Resume Writers, talks to us about interviewing in the zone.

"Truth be known, effective interviewing is nothing more than effective communications. And it's as much about delivery style as it is about content. Here's a key phrase to write down: Interviewing in the zone is not only about what you know, but how you feel about what you know. In other words, you need to be prepared for the questions—yes. But you need to deliver your message with confidence, purpose and passion.

"When athletes are about to perform, what are they thinking about? Are football players studying their playbook before they come out on the field? Are skaters and gymnasts studying their routines before a big performance? No! Peak performing athletes prepare by getting in the zone—mentally! In fact, most coaches will tell you that gold medal performances require NO THINKING at all. Performance time is NOT the time to think—it's the time to become 'instinctively engaged.'

"A young cocky kid named Cassius Clay climbed in the ring in 1964 and against all odds beat the mighty Sonny Liston. Both were prepared physically, but Cassius Clay fought 'in the zone.' You see Clay, who later changed his name to Mohammed Ali, became the 'greatest' because he successfully blended the mental and physical. In fact, more times than not, he psyched out his opponents. And I'm sure you can think of times when the underdog—the team or person with the least talent—won. Why? Because, talent without emotional engagement is wasted energy.

"What does all of this have to do with interviewing for a job? Interviewing is no less a performance than a sporting event. Interviewing is no less a performance than opening night on Broadway. Interviewing is no less a performance than a Presidential Debate. Remember the debate between Kennedy and Nixon? Nixon won according to the few who listened to the debate on radio, but lost in the eyes of the masses who watched it on television. Why? Apparently, Nixon's content was better than Kennedy's, but his physical delivery was inferior. To excel in the interview—to interview in the zone—you have to be well prepared with your material. But more importantly, you must deliver it with energy, enthusiasm, passion and confidence.

"Study communications at any major university and you'll discover that communications is made up of three basic components: (1) Physiology, (2) Tonality and (3) Language (words). 55% of all communications is physiology. 37% is tonality and only 7% is language. So when you prepare for an interview, if you spend 90% of your time rehearsing answers to tough questions, understand that you have invested 90% of your time on something that only makes 7% of the difference. We are told that first impressions are important—dress, proper grooming, a firm handshake, eye contact, a warm smile and so on. Now you know exactly why! Because 55% of all communications is physiology. Physical impressions linger long after the words are forgotten.

"Now remember when our parents told us that it's not what we say, but how we say it? Listen to a speech delivered by a presenter in a monotone voice—and chances are you'll fall asleep. Listen to that same speech delivered by Robin Williams or Whoopi Goldberg, and they'll keep you sitting on the edge of your seat. The lesson here is clear. In order to interview in the zone, you must demonstrate emotion and passion. This doesn't mean you have to be a 'Type A' personality and bounce off the walls. What this does mean is that you fully connect with the interviewers, build rapport and communicate in a way that gets them excited about you and your value to their organization. I advise my clients to listen to their favorite music before an interview—to do whatever they have to do to 'pump themselves up' and to perform at their emotional best. Most people don't interview well because they just don't feel emotionally well going into the interview. They're nervous, uncomfortable and uncertain. Uncertainty is a recipe for disaster. Confidence and control are the keys to success.

"In summary, there is NO substitute for preparation. Know the company you're interviewing with. Be prepared to answer these two questions at the beginning of the interview: (1) What do you know about our company and why do you want to work for us?

(2) What are your skills and qualifications and how do you see them contributing to our organization? Prepare for the tough questions, for sure. But spend more time preparing your delivery. In the end, there are '3 P's' that allow you to interview in the zone: Preparation, purpose and passion. Prepare with a clear purpose—and be sure there is passion, energy and enthusiasm in your delivery. That will separate you from the competition—and then your only problem will be choosing which job offer to accept."

W. Herbert Crowder III, Director of Alumni Career Services, Darden Graduate School of Business Administration at the University of Virginia in Charlottesville, Virginia, writes

"During interviews, many people focus so hard on preparation and on answering the questions being asked that they fail to truly present themselves. A terrific study on communications done at UCLA several years ago broke down effective communications as follows: The words spoken represent only seven percent of the message. Your tonal inflection and body language represent the remaining ninety-three percent. This is how your personality and true self come out in the interview. Remember, you are the message!"

Rebecca Stokes, a Certified Professional Resume Writer and President of The Advantage, Inc., an executive resume and career marketing firm working with clients worldwide from their headquarters in Lynchburg, Virginia, tells us,

"Your resume is the most critical job search tool you have. It is your first introduction to a prospective employer, providing them with information they need to determine whether or not you are a potential candidate. It is also the only physical asset you have to leave behind at the end of an interview to remind a prospective employer of your key career successes. Resumes are designed to be used as a conversation piece, highlighting the challenges, objectives and successes you have achieved throughout your career. If used appropriately, your resume can distinguish you from the crowd, positioning you as the #1 candidate for a highly-regarded, top-paying position.

"During face-to-face interviews, resumes are great presentation tools. If asked about a specific accomplishment or challenge, your resume can help to direct the conversation and allow you to demonstrate your value. Here is an example: You are interviewing for a Chief Operating Officer position with the potential to take over as the next President/CEO in two years. Your resume already highlights your experience as the #2 executive in several unique business environments. In further highlighting your experience you might say, 'I feel comfortable and uniquely qualified to foster a positive relationship as a contemporary and business partner to the President/CEO. In fact, in two of my previous assignments, while I was orchestrating turnaround, rapid growth and market expansion initiatives, I was also being groomed for the top position. It was my responsibility to be both a coach and facilitator, influencing the operating infrastructure while still being careful not to create a bureaucracy or damage the existing corporate culture. Due to the tremendous success attained in such a short period of time, both corporations were subsequently acquired by leading competitors and opportunities for long-term career advancement were limited.'

"In the case of a telephone interview, use your resume as an outline for answering the preliminary questions of an executive recruiter or human resources executive who will be screening you against other applicants. You will also find out the specific requirements for the position and can direct the interviewer's attention to your attributes as they directly relate to the position. You can reaffirm the breadth of your experience in core functional areas, highlighting specific industry or business cultures that are identical to the assignment, or further expand on your accomplishments."

Peter Newfield, President of Retail Search of America in Katonah, New York, writes,

"I always tell people that interviewing is a game and the name of the game is to get a job offer. If you get an offer, then YOU can decide if you want to take it. If you don't get an offer, there is nothing to decide.

"Go into the interview with two kinds of attitudes, regardless of what you think. One is, 'I want this job more than anything in the world and if I don't get it, I'll die.' The other attitude is called humble egotism, which is, 'I'm great, I know I'm great, but I know I have a lot to learn.' If you go in with an attitude of show me why I should work for your company, and halfway through the interview you say to yourself, 'I'd like to work for this company,' it's too late."

Kathryn Jordan, Ph.D., NCCC, Lead Consultant with Drake Beam Morin in Richmond, Virginia, shares,

"The conclusion of all of your pre-work in a job search is the opportunity to interview for a position. The interview is the critical element in any successful career transition. It is in one-on-one contact, whether face-to-face or by telephone, that an employer and potential employee can determine the quality of the matching process for a particular position. Here are several proactive steps you can take to ensure interviewing success.

1. Advance preparation is the 'secret' of interviewing.

2. In many ways, interviewing is an art form. The more you practice, the better you will become. In the interview situation, practice can enhance your performance. This practice should extend to your answers to the interview questions and role playing the actual interviewing process.

3. Complete extensive research about the employer. Find out everything there is to learn about the organization. Try to take a 360 degree approach. Talk to former employees, organizations that compete with the employer, customers of the employer and others. Your goal is to find out not only what trends and products may be impacting the organization, but also to hear the 'insider's perspective' about the organization.

4. Think through how your background fits into this workplace. Do you have similar previous experiences? What skills do you bring that could be useful in this environment? How does your previous training give you an advantage in this organization? What can you do for the organization? How can you help them make money?

5. Identify possible questions and/or objections they may have to your background. Remember, the best defense is always a good offense. Practice your answers to their objections in advance with another listener. Does your answer make sense?

6. Prepare all details. 'The devil is always in the details,' is never as true as in the interview situation. Do not leave anything to chance. For example, you need to think about directions and timing to get to the interview, background information on the people with whom you will be meeting, what to wear, to print extra copies of your resume, etc.

7. Prepare some questions to ask about the position/ employer. Do not ask about salary and benefits, hours, training, etc. However, you can ask things like: 'How will I be evaluated? What are you looking for in the ideal candidate to fill the position? What do you see in the future for the position?' Try to develop several critical questions that you want to have answered by any future employer and utilize those in every interview situation.

8. Follow-up immediately after the interview. Send letters to everyone with whom you spoke. Your goal in your letter should be to either reemphasize how you fit or recoup in any areas where you forgot something critical that may be to your advantage in the hiring decision."

Frank Fox, Executive Director of the Professional Association of Resume Writers in St. Petersburg, Florida, a national association, and the developer of the Certified Professional Resume Writer program tells us,

"Practice first! There are few activities in life that can't be improved with practice, and the 'art' of making a strong impression during a critical job interview is no exception.

"You will have just a few minutes to sell yourself to the decision maker. Therefore, it is important that you are able to present your work history and credentials in a strong verbal presentation. This requires forethought and rehearsal. Prepare to speak in complete sentences and eliminate any 'Uhhhh's' or other 'fillers' from your presentation. Review your resume and be prepared to provide additional information from any aspect of your background that might prompt a question from the interviewer.

"Work on your eye contact and body language. Both can be extremely important in conveying poise and self-confidence expected for $100,000 positions and above. Strive for a balance between relaxed and attentive.

"Prepare answers for some of the 'trick' questions that interviewers like to ask: What did you like least about your previous position? What is your most significant flaw? Having thoughtful answers ready for these delicate questions can contribute greatly to the interviewer's perception of your executive strengths and ability to think quickly.

"A great technique for practicing your interviewing skills is to set up a video camera and have a friend, colleague or spouse interview you several times. Play back the tape and see how you handle each of the points mentioned above. Make a note of the areas that can be improved, then repeat the taped interview process and review it again. Hopefully, you will already see improvement in your delivery by the second effort.

"Continue practicing, as needed, until you feel totally confident and prepared for the real thing."

Debra O'Reilly, President of A First Impression Resume Service in Bristol, Connecticut, and a Certified Professional Resume Writer, writes,

"On my web site is an article concerning interviewing. It is a compilation of wisdom from a variety of sources and reiterates the age-old knowledge that 'appearance communicates an important message about what a candidate has to offer a company. For interviews, dress the part of a professional; wear business clothes.'

"During a telephone interview with an Information Technology client from California, I was reminded that every rule has an exception. The client bluntly informed me that I was offering misinformation within the article; she explained that 'when in Rome, one must do as the Romans do.' In Silicon Valley, she detailed, suits do not rule. If, in fact, an IT professional comes to an interview in Silicon Valley wearing a suit, he/she will often be laughed right out of the door. There, in many companies, 'casual is cool.'

"The truism is this: Appearance does communicate a very important message to the hiring authority. The message you give should be that you understand the working environment well enough to fit in comfortably. So, just as you will research a company's business profile before an interview, also be sure to research patterns of dress and behavior. Over-dressing, you now know, can reduce your chances of success.

"One more stereotype debunked."

Carl Savino, President of Corporate Placements, Inc., a military-to-civilian placement agency in Fairfax Station, Virginia, comments,

"It is critical that you help the interviewer understand the skills and experience you are offering, especially for individuals involved in a career change, such as military service members transitioning back to civilian life. 'Learn the lingo' through active participation in industry associations related to your desired field of employment. Such networking activities are instrumental in gaining the background knowledge needed to translate your work experience in terms relevant to the interviewer."

Wayne Gonyea is an Electronic Career Strategist, developer of numerous career related websites, including Career and Resume Management for the 21st Century and ResumeXPRESS, and President of OnLine Solutions in Morrisonville, New York. He writes,

"Prepare! As much work should be in the preparation as the actual interview. Learn about the company, learn about the position, learn about yourself and practice. Write and rehearse presenting your 3-minute commercial. Forget the hype! Forget any open promises! Hiring agents want to see and hear evidence of accomplishments. They want 'Can Do' people; not 'will do wanna-be's.'

"The Interview: Arrive 5-15 minutes early. Use the restroom; check your appearance. Relax and don't try to cram. Nervous? Practice relaxation techniques like deep breathing and controlled imagery. Wearing winter or rain gear? Remove them and be uncluttered. Carry very little into the interview—only three crisp copies of your resume.

"When you meet the interviewer, make eye contact, shake hands and sit when prompted. Sit with feet flat on the floor, lean slightly forward from the hips, hands on chair arms or in lap. Maintain good eye contact. Smile. Listen carefully to what the interviewer has to say and answer all the questions asked.

"Be serious without being bold. If something is humorous, laugh, but do not project a casual or flippant demeanor.

"Prepare 3-4 questions that demonstrate your knowledge of the position and/or the company. Your questions might also be about promotional opportunities or in-service training. Do not ask about scheduling vacations and other benefit related issues.

"At the end of the interview, thank the interviewer for his/her time, reaffirm your interest in the position and ask what the next step will be. Then, within 48 hours, follow up with a thank you letter on the same paper as your resume.

"**The Psychological Edge:** By following the steps listed above, you will know yourself, the position and the company. You will also know if you are qualified for the position. If you are not, you should not be wasting your time and theirs. Mentally 'move in' to that position. Close your eyes and picture yourself in that position, picture your business cards, your office, your name plate, etc. See yourself in the position!

"Project a 'Can Do' attitude. Know that you are capable of performing the duties of the position and succeeding in the interview. I can do this, I can do this well, I can do this very well!

"Your mental attitude must project the concept that you are 'in control' of the interview. The interviewer will conduct the interview, ask the questions, and ultimately make the decisions, but you are 'in control' and will achieve your goal."

Alesia Benedict, President of Career Objectives Resume Service in Rochelle Park, New Jersey, and Past Executive

Board Member of the Professional Association of Resume Writers, writes,

> "While effective resumes get you in the door ... successful interviewing skills keep you there. Interviews grant you the opportunity to do in-person what your resume did on paper: sell yourself and market your skills to a potential employer. Unfortunately, most job seekers handle the interview the same way as they always have: they wake up, dress in a suit, drive to the interview and answer the questions the interviewer asks with the first thing that comes to their mind. Then they cross their fingers and hope they 'got the job.'

> "Sound familiar?

> "The difference between 'going on' an interview and 'nailing' an interview can be summed up in one word: PREPARATION.

> "The more you know about the company, the position and the general purpose of the corporation for which you are interviewing, the better you can prepare—and the better you prepare, the more you can impress the interviewer and demonstrate how you can contribute to the success of his/her organization. Remember, you must answer their basic (unsaid) question: Why should we hire YOU above all other qualified candidates?

> "It is critical to realize that the person actually conducting the interview isn't always a good interviewer; they may never have been taught how to properly conduct an interview, or they may try to intimidate the candidate in an effort to judge how he/she will react in a pressure situation. They may be having a bad day. They themselves may be up against a deadline. The point is, you don't really know ... so

don't leave it up to the interviewer to (hopefully) ask you the 'right questions' and give you the opportunity to get the vital points of your career and achievements across to the interviewer.

"Know what points you want to emphasize. This means doing your homework. What do you want the interviewer to know about you? Do a complete inventory of your strengths and identify your top three. Then, make sure you work those points into your responses, building on each point with subsequent answers. Use demonstrations to make your point and substantiate your claim. In other words, don't simply say you possess good organizational skills. Provide an example to PROVE you are organized, so that they can VISUALIZE it, making it tangible. 'Good organizational skills' is vague and the interviewer cannot 'see it' in his/her mind. However, when you instead say, 'Perhaps my greatest forte is my organizational skills. For example, we needed to get a key project completed on time, and we were fighting against a difficult deadline. I teamed up with the Department Manager and organized the staff into four teams, each comprised of five staff members. Each group was accountable for a specific aspect of the project: research, production, quality or implementation. The end result was the project was completed two days ahead of schedule, saving the company nearly $25,000. Senior management was clearly impressed.'

"Unfortunately, when asked about their strengths, most candidates will say the first thing that comes to their mind; usually something as lame as: 'I'm definitely a people person and I really work hard.' Think about it: How many people will ever say, 'I'm terribly hostile to others, I take long lunches, and I really don't like it when my boss expects much from me.'

"No one, of course, but if you don't prepare in advance for this question, you will most likely say something equally frivolous as the 'people person' response. Think instead of what you definitely want the interviewer to know: that you successfully developed and implemented your current employer's Y2K disaster recovery plan ... that you achieved 143% of your quota ... that you initiated recertification of ISO 9000, etc.

"Also in your best interest is to pursue as many interviews as you possibly can, even if you have no intention of accepting the position. This gives you the opportunity to 'practice' interviewing and work through your nervousness.

"After each interview, you should send a thank you letter to those persons who interviewed you. Much more than just a way of saying thank you, the letter also serves as an opportunity to 're-sell yourself' to the organization, especially if something went a little amiss.

"As a last bit of advice: Always accept a glass of water or cup of coffee if offered at the onset of the interview. You may be led into the company's kitchen or some other little room, which will immediately transform the interview session into a more relaxed atmosphere, allowing a little chit-chat between you and the interviewer. The cup, by the way, also serves as a wonderful prop and has saved many a job seeker who has gotten off track. Were you just asked a question and are now stumbling to recall the best response? Reach for the cup of water, pause, take a sip, then come back to the question and nail your response!"

Emil Hatz, Managing Director of Hatz International (consultants in sales, marketing and executive search) headquartered in Baltimore, Maryland tells us,

> "I am absolutely amazed how ineffective resumes are from even seasoned executives. It is probably the first glaring mistake most job seekers make because nobody ever showed them how. In 20 years of sales and executive management, I see people miss more opportunities because they have failed to package or present themselves for their target audience.

> "Many initially present their experience in a form that merely describes their functional responsibilities but we already know that. What I counsel candidates to do is list their experiences and then reflect on each one at length to extract those 'impact' activities and achievements that resulted from their actions, leadership or decisions. Tell me what significant improvements were the direct result of your involvement. What's important here is not just the proper and effective packaging of your most important product, but also to prepare yourself to be in the proper frame of mind in an interview, which is to distinguish yourself from the others by being focused on the interviewer's needs and your relative and appropriate 'impact' skills."

Walt Schuette, Certified Professional Resume Writer, Certified Job & Career Transition Coach, and President of The Village Wordsmith in Fallbrook, California, states,

> "Most people express concern when they begin preparing for their job interview. Most job seekers simply do not know what to expect and fear the unknown. That is okay! That is natural. If you are concerned about the interviewing process read on. I will tell

you what you need to know before you go, how to conduct yourself during and what to do after the interview to enhance your chance of selection. It can be easily expressed in three distinct phases—before, during and after.

"To allay some concern, job seekers should approach the job interview from the perspective of having something that the employer wants. Help. You see, the employer would not have advertised the job unless there was a need. Perhaps one of the departments is understaffed or temporarily backed up with too many orders. The HR staffing specialist has asked for help by placing an advertisement. Understand that the reason the interview is being conducted is because the employer needs help. And you are the help. It is difficult to be intimidated by an interviewer when you know that the employer needs you.

"Before you go to the interview, complete this simple checklist. First, review your resume and the job description or job requirements. In your mind, determine what elements in your resume match or closely match the job description. The closer the match the better. If there is no match, you should not be applying for the job. Focus on the jobs for which you are best suited and qualified.

"Next, prepare your wardrobe. You will need at least three different interview outfits. One for the initial interview, the follow-on and the final. Dress for success. That simple statement means that you should dress at least one level better than what you would wear day-in and day-out on the job. Check out the corporate culture (check the parking lot early in the morning and see what people wear to work). Then, dress as well or one step better.

"And finally, put yourself in the interviewer's position. Look at your resume and ask yourself questions that you think the interviewer will ask. Practice your answers. Do not memorize anything, but be prepared to respond to these questions.

"When the actual interview begins, use common sense. Be yourself. There really are only three points to get across. Employers want to know that you can do the job, will do the job and can get along with everyone. Most employers will not directly ask you these three questions—but they will want you to provide the answers.

"Can you do the job? Your resume answers this question for the most part. Nevertheless, at every opportunity during the interview, emphasize that you can.

"Next, at every opportunity display your interest and enthusiasm about the job. Employers want their people to be excited about doing the job.

"Finally, answer the age-old question, 'Do you prefer to work with people or alone?' by making it clear that you prefer to work with people. No one knowingly hires someone who cannot get along with others. If you cannot get along with your co-workers, you will not be offered the job. Simple as that.

"The final three points to emphasize during the interview are these. Employers must understand that you can solve their problems, control costs and increase sales. These three points are crucial to the interview. If you cannot take care of problems, if you increase expenses or cannot favorably influence the profitability of the company, no employer is going to want you on the payroll. Reassure the interviewer that you can, sit back and accept the job offer that follows."

George Crosby, President of the HR Network (publisher of executive job lead reports) in Coopersville, Michigan, and former Vice President of Human Resources for Inryco, Inc. shares the following story.

"Yeah ... I spent nearly two hours with the search consultant who seems like a pro. She's presenting a final slate of candidates to their new CFO within the next two weeks. We really hit it off so I'm sure I'm going to meet him.'

"He received a standard two paragraph letter a month later, thanking him for his interest and lauding the credentials of the 'uniquely well qualified executive' the client selected.

"The guy had sized everything up perfectly, except the outcome. The search consultant did indeed like him a great deal. Nevertheless, when she made the call she decided he was not what her client wanted.

"This little fiction is a composite of scores of experiences of executive job seekers. In it, the candidate let himself get carried away by the chemistry he and the search consultant developed.

"No deception was intended by the consultant. She liked the guy and let it show, but made no allusions to him as an ideal fit for this situation. He drew that conclusion on his own.

"Top-flight search people try to leave a good taste in the mouth of any prospect. It's wise practice, just as it's wise not to substitute their own tastes for those of clients. In a very real sense the consultant is akin to a 'personal shopper,' an advisor/counselor who ultimately respects every client's right to choose what he wants.

"Even the most experienced job hunters are vulnerable to committing a couple of deadly errors:

1. They get too 'up' about attractive jobs. It causes those wearying rides on an emotional roller coaster, in anxiety. Working or not, do your search calmly, seeing yourself as a Cool Hand Luke, with your natural enthusiasm, and disappointments, under firm control.

2. They overestimate the license of strong chemistry with consultants, hiring executives, etc. At a point they lapse into unguarded ease, behaving much too casually during interviews. Among other things, those interviews are professional behavior examinations. Lull yourself into relaxing too much and you run the risk of blowing what you want to portray ... that you're a polished business executive."

Mark Berkowitz, Nationally Certified Career Counselor, Certified Professional Resume Writer, Certified Job & Career Transition Coach, and President of Career Development Resources in Yorktown Heights, New York, shares some of the "pearls" he passes along to his clients.

"(1) Typically, an interview may begin with the ubiquitous 'ice breaker' question, 'So, tell us a little bit about yourself.' While this may seem, on the surface, to be a harmless question, the intent just might go considerably deeper. Oftentimes, the interviewer wants to 'scope out' a candidate and see what his/her priorities happen to be. Should the candidate relate which merit badges he earned in the Scouts? How his college major was selected? Or, should the candidate just plow right ahead and present the 'two minute (four minute)' pitch?

"One tactic that gives the candidate an initial measure of confidence to get the interview off to a good start is to try and determine what the interviewer's hidden agenda is; what is most important to him/ her. The strategy is to respond to the above mentioned question as follows: 'Gee, I'd really love to. Where exactly would you like me to begin?' Now the interviewer must tip the hat and indicate a preference which might just be, 'Oh, let's focus on your current position.'

"No matter whether the candidate begins with his/ her prepared 2-4 minute pitch or receives an indicator as to what the interviewer is most interested in, I counsel them to bring to closure their opening presentation and 'tie everything up with a neat bow.' Candidates finish the presentation with something like this: 'And this brings me to why I'm here today. You see, with my experience and skills, it's obvious that a strong fit exists between what I bring to your organization and what you want or need from the person who is selected for this position.'

"(2) Frequently, my clients are somewhat apprehensive in contemplating certain types of questions which tend to fall into the category, of 'Gosh, I hope they don't ask me _____!' Fill in your own 'silver bullet' question(s). In most cases, these types of questions would reveal information that my clients feel portray weaknesses. I give them a homework assignment, asking them to write down three to five of the questions that they would hope to avoid. We then jointly work out strategies that portray these instances as potential strengths or indicators of 'unique selling features.' Even if these questions are never raised, the candidate goes into the interview with a psychological edge, prepared to demonstrate that he/she is highly qualified and no longer fearful of these types of questions. Being prepared pays off.

"(3) If you don't know what the company's greatest concerns are, it is difficult to sell yourself as the answer to their needs. There are a number of successful strategies to get the interviewer to tell you what the company's special needs are. Some of the questions to ask are: 'If there is one thing that I could do for you in the next 30 days, what would it be?' of 'If you could add or subtract one thing from the incumbent's (previous employee's) performance, what might that be?'"

Margaret "Margy" Porter, Founder of Millennium Associates, an organizational development and business advisory practice in Cary, North Carolina, and past Vice President of Human Resources for Scotland Memorial Hospital, reminds us of some critical issues facing the hiring company. Keep these thoughts in mind in order to better understand and respond to the priorities of the hiring company.

"Whether you are part of an organization or have joined the ranks of independent entrepreneurship, planning for the recruitment process is one of the most important activities you will ever have.

"Optimal success for a line of business, or an entire organization, depends on fit of skills and values to challenges of the job. When I have started the process to hire within an organization or select a contract colleague, one of the most critical tasks is clearly defining the criteria for the job—and the criteria changes over time. Evaluate the vacancy you have now. It is not the same job you may have had several years ago (or even six months ago), and the criteria probably have changed accordingly. Changes in key positions also provide opportunities for re-thinking your current structure. Be your own Devil's Advocate. Should responsibilities be reordered to be more effective in your current competitive environment? In any case, evaluate the job and criteria in 'today's mode.'

"Once you have the appropriate skill essentials in mind, create the advertising to attract the right candidates. Then, develop multiple questions to verify the skills you seek in the interview process. Questions must relate to both interpersonal/communication skills and task/technical skills. 'Fit' also includes values consistent with the organizational culture. For example, if you have an organization with a strong team orientation, a sharing of credit (versus individual contribution) and a predominance of 'stakeholder' problem-solving for decisions, it is imperative to have multiple questions to identify these traits and skills.

"The bottom line is that a great deal of planning is required before you ever get to recruiting, interviewing and selecting. Establish criteria for the job frames the entire process. If you want positive and effective results, put your time in up front in preparation—the rest will then fall into place."

9
Winning in the Next Millennium

The Year 2000 is upon us. For those of us born in the 1930's, 1940's, 1950's and even 1960's, it's hard to believe that so much time has passed. Our parents, if still living, are getting quite elderly, our children are grown, and in fact, many of us are grandparents. We have aged gracefully (I hope!), learned many hard lessons, and become much wiser in our lives, our personal relationships, our business relationships and our careers. The trials and tribulations of our teens and early adult years are far behind. We are more secure with who we are both personally and professionally.

I think back to my college days and the memories are still so fresh. It is difficult to believe that it has been decades since I was there. I think back to my first *"real"* job and the valuable lessons that I learned about being a professional, performing a professional task and delivering professional results. I began to understand how business works, that each player has his/her own agenda, and that positive results require hard work and commitment.

That job, and every one since, have been building blocks, creating the foundation for what I am proud to say has been quite a successful career. Can you look back with the same pride in your successes, contributions and achievements? If you are reading this book, I would assume that your answer is yes. You've had a successful career to date because you have been serious about your profession and now you're serious about your job search. That seriousness, devotion and dedication to a job well done has served you well all of these years and will continue to do so in the future as we enter the next millennium.

What messages did we learn from our parents about being a professional and managing our career? We learned that large corporations provide stability, professional opportunity and the potential for advancement. We learned that if we did a good job, worked hard, demonstrated professional behaviors and delivered strong results, we would be secure. We learned that the company considered us *"family"* and would take care of their own. Most of us launched our careers believing that if we could find the *"right"* company, the *"right"* home, we would be there until retirement.

What a rude awakening many of us had. During our professional lifetimes, the world of corporate employment has changed so dramatically that all of our earlier teachings have been virtually obliterated. As thousands upon thousands of companies have laid off, downsized, rightsized, reengineered and reinvented themselves, so we have had to reinvent our ourselves, rethink our expectations and redefine our objectives. For the 52-year-old aerospace engineer ... the 47-year-old technology sales executive ... the 59-year-old general manager ... and hundreds of thousands of others, the professional legacy our parents left us has disintegrated before our eyes.

As a result, we have been faced with several options:

- Look for another position with a large corporation and *"take our chances"* that the next company would offer more stability.

- Transition our focus to small and midsize companies where we believe that opportunities, albeit more short term, exist.

- Launch an entrepreneurial venture on our own or in partnership with others.

- Transfer our knowledge and experience into the consulting arena.

- Retire, take our money and move to the beach!

If we eliminate the last item from our discussion, all of the others require that we become more educated about our job search. For many of us whose dreams were annihilated, it has been a time of tremendous change, uncertainty, fear and anxiety. Our entire professional lives have built upon one premise that no longer exists. We've had to relearn what our careers are all about and how we could better control them.

Perhaps the most vital lesson that we can have learned is that we cannot look to our employer for security. The sense of *"family"* that was so pervasive in our parent's generation is gone and we have had to learn that the only security in the job market is that which we create for ourselves, from ourselves. That is the reality of the employment market today.

After we have struggled to learn this lesson, it is now time to pass the lesson along to our children and our grandchildren as they embark on their careers. It is our responsibility to teach them how to manage, succeed and prosper in today's dynamic and ever-changing employment market. And not only is it our responsibility to them, it is our responsibility to ourselves. The assumption is made that anyone reading this book is actively engaged in a job search. It is critical that as you teach these lessons, you also learn to live by them and modify your beliefs, expectations and behaviors.

My Challenge To You

My challenge to you is to design your own career and take control of your own destiny. Never again allow yourself to be placed in a position where someone else has such omnipotent influence over your professional life. Realize that you are faced with:

- **Ever increasing and tougher competition**. This is particularly true at the executive level where many individuals have comparable skills and qualifications. What will distinguish you from the crowd is your attitude and your potential *"fit"* with an employer. At your level, you must always remember that companies are not just hiring the professional, but also the person.

- **A greater shift toward self-employment, consulting and interim executive positions** where a company is afforded the luxury of hiring you for a special assignment, project or function without a long-term financial and employment commitment.

- **A greater demand for personal technology skills**. Although in the past many of your technical responsibilities may have been handled by your staff, in the Year 2000 and beyond, many of these responsibilities will be yours. Don't fall behind the curve.

- **A greater thrust on globalization**. Countries and continents once days away are now only seconds away with the emergence of the latest information and telecommunications technologies. Companies are no longer so tightly bound by geographic boundaries. And companies are taking advantage of these opportunities. We must all come to accept this change, appreciate the value of multicultural and multinational organizations, and leverage any and all international experience to our benefit.

How well you are able to respond to these changes in the workplace will dictate your career success—today and in the future. No longer can you be passive, waiting for each new opportunity to present itself to you. You must be clear about your goals and objectives, secure in your professional competencies, successful in marketing your qualifications and proactive in managing your career. If you do not take the lead, someone else will.

Educated job seekers are winners and winners seek new opportunities and new challenges. They have an attitude and aura of success, and are never intimidated by the unknown. They are leaders who take control and move forward, leveraging their past experiences to create new opportunities and achieve new results. These individuals will always be in demand, just as you are today.

By reading this book and devoting the time, energy and resources necessary to your job search, you are already one of the winners. Continued success to you all!

**Never fear change.
Change spurs growth and
growth spurs positive professional performance.**

Index

A

Achievements, 66
Agenda, 4, 17-19
Anxiety, 23
Attitude, 15-16, 72, 122

B

Behavior, 15-16
Benefits:
    employee, 93
    executive, 93-96
Bonuses, 93-94

C

Chemistry, 116
Colleagues, 56
Common ground, 115-116
Communication, 117
Compensation:
    negotiating, 87-102
    requirements, 82
Competition, 6
Computer literacy, 64
Confidence, 27-28
Confidentiality, 100-101
Contracts, 97-101
Contributions, 66-67
Control, 2

D

Deferred compensation
    plans, 95
Deferred contribution
    plans, 95
Dress, 25

E

Education, 6, 70-71
Enthusiasm, 5
Elimination, 8
Equity participation, 95-96
Experts, 114-144

F

Fired, 39-41, 57
Fit, 116
Follow-up:
    letters, 104-110
    telephone, 111-112

G

Goals, 58
Golden handcuffs, 96-97
Golden parachute, 96
Grooming, 25

H
Handshake, 25
Hiring, 33
Honesty, 18
Hours, 79

I
Initiative, 27-28
Innovative, 6
Integrity, 4, 18
Interrogation, 9
Interview (s):
   answers, 49-86
   candidate group, 36-37
   electronic, 31
   face-to-face, 21-22, 32
   informational/net
    working, 29-30
   number of, 22
   obstacles, 39-48
   one-on-one, 34
   out-of-the-office, 37
   panel, 35-36
   participants, 22
   screening, 21, 30-31
   sequential, 35
   serial, 34-35
   telephone, 21
Interviewer, 7-19
Intimidation, 3
Investigate, 7

J
Job fairs, 32

K
Key words
   (see Power words)

L
Letters, 20, 103-110
Listening, 28

M
Marketing, 17
Mentors, 71
Mistakes, 69-70
Motivation, 68

N
Negotiation, 4-5, 87-102
Nervousness, 23
Network, 112-113
Note taking, 20
Notice, 7

O
Objective, 19
Obstacles, 23
Offers, 90-91
Over qualifications, 41-42

P
Performance appraisal,
  56-57
Positives, 26
Power words, 10-14
Practice, 23, 124-125, 129
Preparation, 15-28, 119
Process, 20-22
Problem solving, 60-62

Product, 17-18
Profit sharing, 95
Punctuality, 24-25

Q
Questions:
    asking, 85-86
    direct, 37-38
    illegal, 82-85
    indirect, 38

R
Rapport, 5, 115
Reality, 27
References, 16-17
Research, 8-9
Resignation, 57
Resigning, 98
Risk taking, 69

S
Salary:
    base, 92-93
    negotiating, 87-102
Security, 76-77
Self-confidence, 25
Skills:
    communication, 62-63
    interpersonal, 115
    negotiation, 63-64
Stock options, 94
Strengths, 67
Stress, 3-4, 65-66
Style:
    decision making, 60
    leadership, 59

management, 59
Success, 64-65
Subordinates, 56
Supervisor, 55-56, 72-73

T
Termination, 99
Thank you (see Letters)
Transcend, 7-8
Travel, 79
Trust, 5

U
Unemployed, 45-47

V
Validating, 9
Value, 57-58
Vitality, 5-6

W
Weaknesses, 67-68
Winning, 6

Career Resources

Contact Impact Publications for a free annotated listing of career resources or visit the World Wide Web for a complete listing of career resources: www.impactpublications.com. The following career resources are available directly from Impact Publications. Complete the following form or list the titles, include postage (see formula at the end), enclose payment, and send your order to:

IMPACT PUBLICATIONS
9104-N Manassas Drive
Manassas Park, VA 20111-5211
Tel 1-800/361-1055, 703/361-7300, or Fax 703/335-9486

Quick and easy online ordering: *www.impactpublications.com*

Qty.	Titles	Price	Total
INTERVIEWS			
	101 Dynamite Answers to Interview Questions	12.95	
	101 Dynamite Questions to Ask at Your Job Interview	14.95	
	111 Dynamite Ways to Ace Your Job Interview	13.95	
	Complete Q & A Job Interview Book	14.95	
	Conquer Interview Objectives	10.95	
	Haldane's Best Answers to Tough Interview Questions	15.95	
	Information Interviewing	10.95	
	Interview for Success	15.95	
	Interview Power	12.95	
	Job Interviews for Dummies	12.99	
	Job Interviews That Mean Business	12.00	
	Killer Interviews	10.95	
	Savvy Interviewer	10.95	
	Winning Interviews for $100,000+ Jobs	17.95	
RESUMES & LETTERS			
	$100,000 Resume	16.95	
	100 Winning Resumes for $100,000+ Jobs	24.95	
	101 Best Resumes	10.95	
	101 Quick Tips for a Dynamite Resume	13.95	
	1500+ Key Words for $100,000+ Jobs	14.95	
	175 High-Impact Resumes	10.95	
	America's Top Resumes for America's Top Jobs	19.95	
	Asher's Bible of Executive Resumes	29.95	
	Best Resumes for $75,000+ Executive Jobs	14.95	
	Complete Idiot's Guide to Writing the Perfect Resume	16.95	
	Conquer Resume Objections	10.95	
	Dynamite Resumes	14.95	
	Electronic Resumes and Online Networking	13.99	
	Encyclopedia of Job-Winning Resumes	16.95	
	Gallery of Best Resumes	16.95	
	Gallery of Best Resumes for Two-Year Degree Graduates	16.95	
	Haldane's Best Resumes for Professionals	15.95	
	Heart & Soul Resumes	15.95	
	High Impact Resumes and Letters	19.95	
	Resume Catalog	15.95	
	Resume Magic	18.95	
	Resume Shortcuts	14.95	

_____	Resumes for the Over-50 Job Hunter	14.95 _____
_____	Resumes for Re-Entry	10.95 _____
_____	Resume Winners from the Pros	17.95 _____
_____	Resumes for Dummies	12.99 _____
_____	Resumes That Knock 'Em Dead	10.95 _____
_____	Savvy Resume Writer	10.95 _____
_____	Sure-Hire Resumes	14.95 _____

COVER LETTERS

_____	101 Best Cover Letters	11.95 _____
_____	175 High-Impact Cover Letters	10.95 _____
_____	200 Letters for Job Hunters	19.95 _____
_____	201 Winning Cover Letters for the $100,000+ Jobs	24.95 _____
_____	201 Dynamite Job Search Letters	19.95 _____
_____	201 Killer Cover Letters	16.95 _____
_____	Complete Idiot's Guide to the Perfect Cover Letters	14.95 _____
_____	Cover Letters for Dummies	12.99 _____
_____	Cover Letters that Knock 'Em Dead	10.95 _____
_____	Dynamite Cover Letters	14.95 _____
_____	Gallery of Best Cover Letters	18.95 _____
_____	Haldane's Best Cover Letters for Professionals	15.95 _____

INTERNET JOB SEARCH/HIRING

_____	Career Exploration On the Internet	15.95 _____
_____	Electronic Resumes	19.95 _____
_____	Employer's Guide to Recruiting on the Internet	24.95 _____
_____	Guide to Internet Job Search.	14.95 _____
_____	Heart & Soul Internet Job Search	16.95 _____
_____	How to Get Your Dream Job Using the Web	29.99 _____
_____	Internet Resumes	14.95 _____
_____	Job Searching Online for Dummies	24.99 _____
_____	Resumes in Cyberspace	14.95 _____

ALTERNATIVE JOBS & EMPLOYERS

_____	100 Great Jobs and How To Get Them	17.95 _____
_____	101 Careers	16.95 _____
_____	Best Jobs for the 21st Century	19.95 _____
_____	Careers in Computers	17.95 _____
_____	Careers in Health Care	17.95 _____
_____	Careers in High Tech	17.95 _____
_____	Cool Careers for Dummies	16.95 _____
_____	Cybercareers	24.95 _____
_____	Directory of Executive Recruiters	44.95 _____
_____	Hidden Job Market 2000	18.95 _____
_____	High-Skill, High-Wage Jobs	19.95 _____
_____	JobBank Guide to Computer and High-Tech Companies	16.95 _____
_____	Media Companies 2000	18.95 _____
_____	Sunshine Jobs	16.95 _____
_____	Top 2,500 Employers 2000	18.95 _____
_____	What Employers Really Want	14.95 _____
_____	You Can't Play the Game If You Don't Know the Rules	14.95 _____

RECRUITERS/EMPLOYERS

_____	Adams Executive Recruiters Almanac	16.95 _____
_____	Directory of Executive Recruiters	44.95 _____
_____	Employer's Guide to Recruiting on the Internet	24.95 _____
_____	Job Seekers Guide to Executive Recruiters	34.95 _____

JOB STRATEGIES AND TACTICS

101 Ways to Power Up Your Job Search	12.95	
24 Hours to Your Next Job, Raise, or Promotion	10.95	
Career Bounce-Back	14.95	
Career Chase	17.95	
Career Intelligence	15.95	
Career Starter	10.95	
Complete Idiot's Guide to Changing Careers	17.95	
Executive Job Search Strategies	16.95	
Five Secrets to Finding a Job	12.95	
Get Ahead! Stay Ahead!	12.95	
Getting from Fired to Hired	14.95	
How to Get Interviews from Classified Job Ads	14.95	
How to Succeed Without a Career Path	13.95	
How to Make Use of a Useless Degree	13.00	
Is It Too Late To Run Away and Join the Circus?	14.95	
Job Hunting in the 21st Century	17.95	
Job Hunting Made Easy	12.95	
Knock 'Em Dead 1999	12.95	
Me, Myself, and I, Inc.	17.95	
New Rights of Passage	29.95	
No One Is Unemployable	29.95	
Perfect Pitch	13.99	
Professional's Job Finder	18.95	
Reinventing Your Career	9.99	
Resumes Don't Get Jobs	10.95	
So What If I'm 50	12.95	
Staying in Demand	12.95	
Strategic Job Jumping	13.00	
Take Yourself to the Top	13.99	
Top 10 Career Strategies for the Year 2000 & Beyond	12.00	
Top 10 Fears of Job Seekers	12.00	
What Employers Really Want	14.95	
Who Says There Are No Jobs Out There	12.95	
Work Happy Live Healthy	14.95	

TESTING AND ASSESSMENT

Career Satisfaction and Success	14.95	
Career Tests	12.95	
Dictionary of Holland Occupational Codes	45.00	
Discover the Best Jobs For You	14.95	
Discover What You're Best At	12.00	
Making Vocational Choices	29.95	
Real People, Real Jobs	15.95	

ATTITUDE & MOTIVATION

Ways to Motivate Yourself	15.99	
Attitude Is Everything	14.99	
Change Your Attitude	15.99	
Reinventing Yourself	18.99	

INSPIRATION & EMPOWERMENT

Do What You Love, the Money Will Follow	11.95	
Doing Work You Love	14.95	
Emotional Intelligence	13.95	
Getting Unstuck	11.99	
If It's Going To Be, It's Up To Me	22.00	
If Life Is A Game, These Are the Rules	15.00	
Love Your Work and Success Will Follow	12.95	

_____	Power of Purpose	20.00	_____
_____	Seven Habits of Highly Effective People	14.00	_____
_____	To Build the Life You Want, Create the Work You Love	10.95	_____

ETIQUETTE AND IMAGE

_____	Business Etiquette and Professionalism	10.95	_____
_____	Dressing Smart in the New Millennium	13.95	_____
_____	Executive Etiquette in the New Workplace	14.95	_____
_____	First Five Minutes	14.95	_____
_____	John Molloy's Dress for Success (For Men)	13.99	_____
_____	New Professional Image	12.95	_____
_____	New Women's Dress for Success	12.99	_____
_____	Red Socks Don't Work	14.95	_____
_____	Winning Image	17.95	_____
_____	You've Only Got 3 Seconds	22.95	_____

NETWORKING

_____	Dynamite Networking for Dynamite Jobs	15.95	_____
_____	Dynamite Tele-Search	12.95	_____
_____	Effective Networking	10.95	_____
_____	Great Connections	11.95	_____
_____	How to Work a Room	11.99	_____
_____	Power Schmoozing	12.95	_____
_____	Power To Get In	24.95	_____

SALARY NEGOTIATIONS

_____	Dynamite Salary Negotiations	15.95	_____
_____	Get a Raise in 7 Days	14.95	_____
_____	Get More Money on Your Next Job	14.95	_____
_____	Negotiate Your Job Offer	14.95	_____

☞ **SUBTOTAL** $ _____

☞ Virginia residents add 4½% sales tax) _____

☞ Shipping/handling, Continental U.S., $5.00 + $5.00
plus following percentages when **SUBTOTAL** is:

□ $30-$100—multiply SUBTOTAL by 8% _____

□ $100-$999—multiply SUBTOTAL by 7% _____

□ $1,000-$4,999—multiply SUBTOTAL by 6% _____

□ Over $5,000—multiply SUBTOTAL by 5% _____

☞ □ If shipped outside Continental US, add another 5% _____

☞ **TOTAL ENCLOSED** $ _____

SHIP TO: (street address only for UPS or RPS delivery)

Name _____

Address _____

_____

_____

Telephone _____

I enclose ❑ Check ❑ Money Order in the amount of: $ _____

Charge $_____ to ❑ Visa ❑ MC ❑ AmEx

Card # _____ Exp: _____ / _____

Signature _____

Discover Hundreds of Additional Resources on the World Wide Web!

Looking for the newest and best books, directories, newsletters, wall charts, training programs, videos, computer software, and kits to help you land a job, negotiate a higher salary, or start your own business? Want to learn the most effective way to find a job in Asia or relocate to San Francisco? Are you curious about how to find a job 24 hours a day using the Internet or about what you'll be doing five years from now? Are you trying to keep up-to-date on the latest career resources, but are not able to find the latest catalogs, brochures, or newsletters on today's "best of the best" resources?

Welcome to the first virtual career bookstore on the Internet. Now you're only a click away with Impact Publications' electronic solution to the resource challenge. Visit this rich site to quickly discover everything you ever wanted to know about finding jobs, changing careers, and starting your own business—including many useful resources that are difficult to find in local bookstores and libraries. The site also includes what's new and hot, tips for job search success, and monthly specials. Check it out today!

www.impactpublications.com